Culture and Diversity
Stories for Work and Life

SUNNIVA HEGGERTVEIT-AOUDIA

Dear Simon,
Sending you the "first edition" of the paperback version. The transfer from Kindle to CreateSpace caused a few hich-ups, so this version has 82 technical faults.... Don't look too closely!

Thanks for your help.
Sunniva

Copyright © 2015 Sunniva Heggertveit-Aoudia

Language editor: Simon Marshall-Jones

Photo editor: Delphine Baron

All rights reserved.

ISBN: 295529991X
ISBN-13: 978-2955299913

CONTENTS

PREFACE: THE TALE ABOUT THE ELEPHANT AND THE BLIND MEN

CHAPTER ONE: THE JOURNEY TO DIVERSITY AND INCLUSION — 1
- WHY THIS BOOK? — 1
- EARLY AWAKENING — 3
- NORWEGIAN HERITAGE, VIKING TRAVELER'S BLOOD? — 3
- A BRIEF ANECDOTE ABOUT HERITAGE AND NORWEGIAN HISTORY — 4
- CURRENT MEDITERRANEAN LIFE — 5
- BEING AN ENTREPRENEUR — 6

CHAPTER TWO: WHAT IS "DIVERSITY AND INCLUSION" ANYWAY? — 9

CHAPTER THREE: DIVERSITY AND UNIFORMITY — 11
- DIVERSITY AROUND THE WORLD — 12
- DIVERSITY OR DIFFERENCES IN DAILY LIFE — 14
- FINAL REMARKS — 17

CHAPTER FOUR: ZOOMING IN ON NATIONAL CULTURE — 19
- CULTURAL VALUES — 21
- INDIVIDUAL VERSUS GROUP VALUES — 23
- NATIONAL IDENTITY, THE FEELING OF "ME" — 24
- SUCCESSFUL CROSS-CULTURAL TEAMS — 27
- GIVING FEEDBACK; WHAT LENSES DO YOU WEAR? — 29
- LANGUAGE: WHAT IS EFFICIENT COMMUNICATION? — 32
- ADAPTING TO A CULTURE, DOES IT MEAN FORGETTING YOUR OWN? — 33
- IMMIGRATION VERSUS CROSS-CULTURE — 35

WORK-LIFE BALANCE IN A GLOBAL CONTEXT	41
PRESENTATION SKILLS SEEN THROUGH A CULTURAL VIEW	43
CULTURAL DIFFERENCES, WOMEN AND MEN	45
NATIONAL CULTURE AND THE PEOPLE MAGNET	46
FINAL REMARKS	49

CHAPTER FIVE: GENDER AND FREEDOM — 51

WHAT IF…	57
BURQA AND NIQAB BAN IN FRANCE	59
SOMETIMES WE JUST NEED SOMEONE TO SHED LIGHT ON A SITUATION	62
AFFAIRE DSK: POSITIVE EFFECTS	63
FROGS, PEOPLE AND HOT WATER	64
DANCE A NEW DANCE?	65
A NEW ERA OF WOMEN ENTREPRENEURS?	69
COSMETIC SURGERY, FREEDOM AND WOMEN	72
STEREOTYPING AND UNCONSCIOUS BIAS CAUSED BY ADVERTISEMENTS	73
WOMEN AND SERENITY, OR RATHER, LACK OF	75
FINAL REMARKS	77

CHAPTER SIX: GENERATIONS OR CHANGING TIMES — 81

ZAPPING LIVES	81
WORK LESS, EARN MORE?	84
GENERATIONS AND HAPPINESS	86
LIVING THE DREAM	88
FINAL REMARKS	90

CHAPTER SEVEN: NO DIVERSITY WITHOUT INCLUSION — 93

INCLUSIVE BEHAVIOURS AND THE TIME SQUEEZE	94
THE POWER OF WORDS	96
WALK IN SOMEONE ELSE'S SHOES	98

GETTING OUT OF YOUR COMFORT ZONE - WHAT DOES IT MEAN?	100
DO YOU SEE PEOPLE?	102
GIVING SPACE	103
HIGH-PERFORMING TEAMS OR HAPPY TEAMS?	104
LANGUAGE AS AN INCLUSIONAL TOOL	106
SEEING BEYOND	108
INCLUSIVE BEHAVIOURS AND SEEING THINGS IN A WIDER CONTEXT	110
INSPIRATION, CREATIVITY, MINDFULNESS	111
AN LGBT INCLUSIVE WORK ENVIRONMENT	113
HIDDEN DISABILITY	117
« IT WOULD HAVE BEEN BETTER IF MY ARM HAD BEEN CUT OFF…	118
UNDERGROUND OR NOT TO UNDERGROUND?	121
INCLUSION FOR PEOPLE WITH HEARING IMPAIRMENT	122
SEEING OPPORTUNITIES WHERE OTHER'S DON'T	124
FINAL REMARKS	125

CHAPTER EIGHT: THAT'S ALL, FOLKS — 127

CHAPTER NINE: FOR STUDENTS AND DISCUSSION GROUPS — 129

CHAPTER TEN: TOOLKIT: INCLUSIONAL ACTIVITIES FOR REFLECTION — 131

UNDERSTANDING YOUR OWN CULTURE	131
UNDERSTANDING OTHERS	132
PROMOTING INCLUSION AND COMMITMENT IN TEAMS	132
PROMOTING A LARGE IN-GROUP	133

ABOUT THE AUTHOR	135
ACKNOWLEDGMENTS	137
REFERENCES AND LINKS OF INTEREST	139

PREFACE:
THE TALE ABOUT THE ELEPHANT AND THE BLIND MEN

You have most likely seen the picture on the cover in some format, and you might have heard about this story. I chose the image because it symbolises the content of this book; there are many views of the same thing and we don't always have the entire overview. Knowing that, might make us more humble and curious.

I have come across this story several times in my professional career, but I didn't know that it came from India before I started doing some research on the internet. According to Wikipedia, the tale has many versions and is known and mentioned in several religions; notably Jain (Indian religion), Buddhism, Sufism (Islam) and Hinduism. John Godrey Saxe (1816 - 1887) wrote a poem on the story in the 19th century and by this means made it known in Europe.

This particular story summary is taken, with permission, from the organisation Wild Equus - Equilibre Gaia in Tarragona, Spain. They work on promoting a better understanding of equines, their behaviour and the horse-human relationship.

"The parable of the blind men and the elephant is used to illustrate how biases can blind us, preventing us from seeking a more complete understanding on the nature of things. It is often used as a warning against the promotion of absolute truths.

"The story of the blind men and an elephant originated in India (Pali Buddhist Udana) from where it is widely diffused. Made famous by the great Sufi master Jalal ad-Din Rumi (1207-1273 c.e.) in his Mathnawi of Jalalu'ddin Rumi, the parable has been used to illustrate a range of truths and fallacies.

"The parable went something like this:

« In a distant village, a long time ago, there lived six blind men. One day the villagers announced, 'Hey, there is an elephant in the village today.'

"They had never seen or felt an elephant before and so decided, 'Even though we would not be able to see it, let us go and feel it anyway.' And thus they went down to the village to touch and feel the elephant to learn what animal this was and they described it as follows:

'Hey, the elephant is a pillar,' said the first man who touched his leg.

'Oh, no! it is like a rope,' argued the second after touching the tail.

'Oh, no! it is like a thick branch of a tree,' the third man spouted after touching the trunk.

'It is like a big hand fan' said the fourth man feeling the ear.

'It is like a huge wall,' sounded the fifth man who groped the bell.

'It is like a solid pipe,' said the sixth man with the tusk in his hand.

"They all fell into heated argument as to who was right in describing the big beast, all sticking to their own perception. A wise sage happened to hear the argument, stopped and asked them 'What is the matter?' They said, 'We cannot agree to what the elephant is like.'

"The wise man then calmly said, 'Each one of you is correct; and each one of you is wrong. Because each one of you had only touched a part of the elephant's body. Thus you only have a partial view of the animal. If you put your partial views together, you will get an idea of what an elephant looks like.'

"At various times it has provided insight into the relativity, opaqueness or inexpressible nature of truth, the behaviour of experts in fields where there is a deficit or inaccessibility of information, the need for communication, and respect for different perspectives.

"Although the parable's function is to call attention to a lack of objectivity and consideration of other approaches and perspectives when trying to understand the nature of things, we do have to warn that not all perspectives are equally valid, and even valid arguments are not necessarily equally sound.

"Each of us lives in our own world, with our own life experiences and sensory perceptions, which often lead us to biases characterized by a lack of general objectivity, open-mindedness or the consideration of the points of view of others.

"In a world where issues are usually and uncritically two sided: black or white: good or bad; ethical or unethical, it is easy to fall into heated debates, each defending a point of view often times equated to truths.

"The elephant in this sense represents reality, and each of the worthy blind sages represents a different approach to understanding this reality. In all objectivity, all the sages have correctly described their piece of reality, but fail by arguing that their reality is the only truth."

Some phrases stand out for me, which are relevant to this book;

- All of you are right (and no one is wrong). You only have a partial view of the elephant, if you put the pieces together, you will get an idea of the whole picture.
- The need for objectivity, communication and respect for differences.
- We are biased by our own experiences (and upbringing).
- The importance of considering all viewpoints and the manifold nature of truth. Truth can be stated in different ways. There is no absolute truth.

All these statements are important when collaborating with others, maybe particularly so if you live and work with different nationalities. Many of us grow up in one national culture, which leads us to having a cultural filter on how we view the world, and by that we become biased on what is good/bad and right/wrong. In a complex world we will benefit from being open minded, consider several view points and take a position of objectivity before deciding what is *the truth*.

CULTURE AND DIVERSITY

CHAPTER ONE:
THE JOURNEY TO DIVERSITY AND INCLUSION

Why This Book?

Many a time people have told me I should write a book, but it was mostly related to my travels and life experiences. When I worked at a large international enterprise in the first decade of the 2000s, I used to create newsletters for the Human Resources (HR) and Diversity & Inclusion (D&I) population I worked with. I got a lot of feedback saying that people enjoyed my newsletters and some outside of that population contacted me wishing to be added to my distribution list. It was my first experience in writing for an audience and I truly enjoyed it.

Starting my own business some years later, I was advised to write blogs to get traffic to my site. Since I enjoy writing and I feel passionately about what I do, I thought it was a good idea. Feedback started to come in that my blogs made people reflect. And again, people said; "Why don't you write a book?" I then started thinking that storytelling could be a way to convey my message. "Oblique learning", as writer John Kay might say. (In Kay's book he explains why indirect methods may be more effective, for instance "Why objectives often are best pursued indirectly" or "How the world is too complex for directness to be direct".)

Writing a book does feel like going out on a limb, though. What do *I* have to offer *you* as a reader?

I want to contribute to a more inclusive workplace and society through the medium of this book by sharing examples, reflections and short stories, the underlying message being that we will be better off if we can embrace diversity fully. And we embrace through inclusion. I also invite you to make your own reflections: how would *you* solve the various situations, what do *you* think?

This book is pragmatic and conversational; I think we all tend to remember a theory or idea better when there is a story attached. Teachers and presenters often personalize the theory or add a story about someone so that you are more likely to recall it. Additionally, research (e.g. by American economist Paul J. Zak) has shown that stories trigger our empathic skills and therefore we are more likely to understand how others might react. This is very useful in a globalized world.

You will find that there are many pictures in this book that tell their own stories, or underline a point in the text. Pictures, like stories, tend to make information "stick" in our minds, especially for the visual learners among us.

I hope my book will inspire you to ponder, learn, remember, formulate ideas, and maybe do things differently. I hope it also makes you smile and sometimes nod in recognition of your own experiences. It is a serious subject, but I think we can manage challenges and serious subjects better with a bit of humour. This is a book as much for life at work as for life in general. We meet diversity, different viewpoints, and different ways of living everywhere. Keeping an open mind and trying to put oneself in someone else's shoes - that's inclusion. We are challenged in these areas anywhere and everywhere.

The book is a medley of my blogs, some articles I wrote for the magazine *Diversity Journal* in the US and my reflections as a Norwegian, a woman and a D&I practitioner. It envisages my life in diversity and inclusion, my perspectives, my bird's eye view. Keeping that in mind, you will at times notice my Norwegian cultural filter, particularly on egalitarianism. The stories on culture are also seen through the glasses of a European; I therefore talk about nationality, not race. To enrich the reading experience, I invited some people from various countries to share a story of their own. We all have them; maybe this book will bring out your own memories which you can use to make a point in a discussion or a presentation.

Early Awakening

I remember well when I first discovered gender inequality. I was seven years old.

My three elder brothers, whom I adored, always seemed to have a lot of fun, and they wore blue jeans. My mother kept on forcing me to wear dresses, of which the pink colour was my absolute nightmare. She also told me to stay clean. From this I made the logical conclusion that life was: For boys - they can wear jeans, get dirty, and have fun. Girls - they should wear dresses, should stay clean: in other words, no fun! What an injustice!

The journey of diversity and inclusion had begun...

Norwegian Heritage, Viking Traveler's Blood?

I am a born and bred Norwegian. I grew up in the southern parts of Norway - with a short stay of a year in the west. I lived in various towns, as you will see from the map on the next page. My father's family stem from the valley Setesdal, which is south/inland, and were mostly farmers. My grandfather, however, was a teacher, one who refused to talk about the Nazi ideology in a positive manner and therefore was jailed and sent north to the Russian border in a forced-labour camp. He survived the camp, but died soon after returning home. The rumour was that the Germans put small pieces of glass in the prisoners' food to make their death slow and painful. My grandmother managed to find food for her four children during the war, mostly potatoes, turnips and berries - and my father still loves potatoes, strangely enough!

My mother's family is from the west, a valley outside of Bergen, many of the inhabitants farmers and some with political interests. Her father owned a wood factory, while her mother worked as a seamstress in her later years. The people of the west are mixed with European blood due to centuries of commercial activities with Europe (yes, Vikings too). Many members of my mother's family are short, have brown eyes and black or red hair. Not a very Scandinavian look.

I very early in life I picked up a taste for travels and curiosity about foreign lands and foreign people. Was it my mother's stories about her possible heritage from the Nordic branch of gypsies (called *Tater*) and French people? Or maybe it was my stepfather's stories about his travels in

Europe in the 60s and 70s?

On that note, I can still remember my stepfather's story from Marseille in France (where I now live). Walking through town he all of a sudden saw a bar with this note on the door: "Forbidden for Norwegians and Negroes".

A Brief Anecdote About Heritage and Norwegian History

When it comes to women's rights, the introduction of Christianity around year 1000 was not good news for the Norwegian women in Viking times. Slowly, but surely, women lost their original rights and value, as Christianity became the principal religion.

What were their rights? Historians and scholars are starting to read the archeological signs differently. Recent research, e.g. around the ships *Osebergskipene*, now shows that the two rich women buried in these ships were important in themselves, not as "wives of". The roles were different, in that most warrior Vikings were men and the women were the "key keepers" of the house. Women also came along on raids as warriors, but they were few. Mostly the Viking woman was in charge of all practical issues when her husband was away. She had the right to divorce, and she kept all her property. There were women merchants and women interpreting religion (*volve*, these were also seen to be clairvoyants).

Norway was not alone in having had a more women-friendly religion pre-Christianity. According to archeologist Dr Marija Gimbuta (revised version of *Gods and Goddesses in Old Europe, 7000 - 3500 B.C.*), old Europe was based on a matriarchal culture where the mother goddess had an important role in society.

The Nordic countries (Norway, Denmark, Sweden, Iceland and Finland) are the most egalitarian countries in the world, which tells me that even though external factors contributed to bringing down women's importance in society via Christianity, the root culture still remained - women have kept a more equal role in society compared to many others.

Current Mediterranean Life

After having lived in Switzerland, Cyprus and Texas I ended up stranded in southern France, nearby Marseille - the city that didn't like Norwegians and Negroes. Today it's rather the Roma people that frustrate the citizens of Marseille. But before that it was the North Africans and before that the Italians. Marseille has an exotic history; it is a city that has seen many waves of immigration. And that's where I have landed, although not bringing a Norwegian immigration wave, there are not many of us around...

At the beginning I was disappointed at the lack of international food. I was used to buying "world food" in supermarkets, having a vegetarian choice at restaurants and "fusion food" from different nationalities. I didn't consider that I had moved to the place of "French Cuisine", a country very proud of its food culture. About a year later a friend of mine asked: "You are so close to Italy, you probably have that savory hard cheese with pepper, right? Can you bring that to Norway next time?" I laughed and said: "You tell me to bring an Italian cheese from The Country of Cheese??!!" I had integrated.

Marseille is also part of the Mediterranean culture, which is rather traditional. I'm a feminist in macho land, someone from the most egalitarian country in the world. How did that happen? Love, what else! My dear husband is French and grew up in this region. We met at work, both of us in international jobs in a large international company. And when his expat assignment came to an end, he cunningly said; "You know how much I have struggled to learn English, imagine what an effort it would be for me to learn Norwegian! You are so good at languages, you can easily learn French". Oh dear. Therefore, I started learning French and we moved to France six months later.

And what a culture shock it was! I remember my first big family lunch. All the women cooked, ran between the tables, served and cleaned. And the men sat back and enjoyed being served. I was horrified! (I still am) Or when the first tax statement arrived. I had not changed my name after marriage, but the state did it for me, so all of a sudden I was Madame HUSBAND'S LAST NAME, HUSBAND'S FIRST NAME. I was angry for two weeks...

Being an Entrepreneur

After ten years in international roles in a large enterprise, working with people from around the globe, I decided it was time to do my own thing. I had learned so much, I had grown as a human resources professional and I had become a specialist within diversity and inclusion.

On that note, I had literally "hunted" for a job in D&I with my previous employer, as I felt more meaning in the tasks that related to D&I. I strongly felt - and had experienced - the usefulness of a diverse workforce, and also saw the need for people pushing others towards diversity. I suppose I was also attracted to this profession because I had always been "different" somehow; as a girl who grew up with brothers, as a vegetarian, as someone who didn't like the general strive for "uniformity" or having to be or look a certain way according to societal pressures.

Being self-employed had been at the back of my mind for about eight years before it actually happened. I was attracted to being completely in charge, being allowed to focus on my strengths and my creativity, to be able to implement ideas right away, and to running my own schedule. Having worked for a while in a large business, I was slightly tired of the administrative tasks and the reporting needed. And, frankly speaking: managers. As member of a minority culture (Norwegian or even Scandinavian), I always had to adapt to the culture of my superior, and in the end I started finding that tiring. I have an egalitarian attitude and several other cultures find that threatening, I realised, when it comes from a subordinate.

I entered a new world. My very first impression was that so many people wanted my advice and experience for free, which I gave willingly at first, but it was not a good business model.... When I put a frame around what I was willing to give for free and what I would expect payment for, things changed, however. Then I met the most generous people, and I feel grateful to be in this world of entrepreneurs.

This is how I got here, to write this book. Before starting the next chapter, what is your story? Why are you where you are? What made you make these choices?

CHAPTER TWO:
WHAT IS "DIVERSITY AND INCLUSION" ANYWAY?

Before we get to my stories, I would like to be clear on what we are talking about. I personally see the term *Diversity and Inclusion* as an umbrella for a variety of subjects.

Simply said, *Diversity* is all the ways we differ, or how we are different from one another. One can say it is "who we are"; our human qualities and our history. We often talk about dimensions of diversity, which could be age, gender, ethnicity, race, physical abilities, and sexual orientation. Many companies, depending on local laws, measure this kind of diversity. Diversity in a team could also be; educational background, geographic location, marital status, military experience, parental status, religion, and work experience. You might also have heard of 'diversity of thought'; an example being team members with similar backgrounds but with very different outlooks on challenges and how to solve them.

Which takes us to the word *Inclusion*; interestingly enough it is a word and terminology that cannot be translated into the other languages I use daily; Norwegian and French. You can't have a successful diverse workplace or society without inclusion. One could say that *Inclusion* binds it all together and it is also *how we work together*. This is where an open mind, curiosity, tolerance, and willingness to understand play important roles. An inclusive environment makes people feel part of the 'in-group' and that they belong (more about in-groups in the chapter on inclusion). Several studies (IMD Business School, Stanford Business School) show that a diverse team outperform a homogeneous team, but only if there is an inclusive mindset among its team members.

In business we talk about *diversity and inclusion* as one, but as you see from the descriptions above, the words mean very different things - they are however dependent on each other. Thing is, we tend to choose people who are like us, whether it is the same gender, same nationality, or maybe the same background (university, military service, etc). What is similar, seems *safe*, we know what we get - pretty much. However, it is not good for business, as several studies have proved; we miss out on innovation and different solutions (more about this later). It is not only in business, of course - students from abroad stick to the same nationality, similarly with immigrants. The upside is a feeling of safety; the downside is that people don't learn the language and the culture of where they find themselves. Students miss out on learning other perspectives. Because of this tendency to choose *uniformity* we need people to remind us of the necessity and advantages of D&I. That's why we need books like this one.

In this book, I will briefly touch on the general subject of diversity, then concentrate on two dimensions of it; national culture and gender, before closing out with a look on generations. In the chapter on Inclusion, I will discuss several areas of diversity, as Inclusion is all encompassing of diversity in our lives - this is for me a 'potpourri chapter'.

CHAPTER THREE:
DIVERSITY AND UNIFORMITY

The first time I really lived and understood the need for diversity was when I worked as a recruiter in the late 1990s. All kinds of skills and ages were needed, for example the person who was happy with, and good at, registering numbers all day, who worked on projects for years; or the 70-year-old lady who was our most popular receptionist.

As a recruiter I learnt to appreciate the complexity of a society's needs, and that all of us have a role to play, whatever interests and competences. Additionally, I had my first experience of seeing in practice the advantages of mixing strengths and personalities in a team. We worked in duos; one consultant with more focus on the business clients, one consultant more focused on hiring personnel. During one period I was working in a duo where we together represented charm and knowledge (I wasn't the charmer...); a very strong combination when doing client visits. I was resistant at first, because, honestly speaking, I didn't think my colleague was very skilled in our profession. But, to my own surprise, I noticed how we always came back from client visits with more business. My colleague 'warmed them up' with charm and small-talk, and I added the professional bit. It really worked!

This is also where I met discrimination. I will never forget a customer who had contacted us to get temporary help in their reception. He asked; "How black is she?" when I proposed a lady with an African name. Let's just pause here. He asked; "How black is she?" I was shocked and angry. I didn't want to send the lady with the African name to this company, and I made a note in our internal system that this customer should not receive any service from us, as it would be against our values. Another example of discrimination is that I realized it worked better to present the education and work experience of a foreign candidate first, and give the name only when the customer had accepted. Otherwise they found reasons for saying no. I was appalled by this injustice, and my eyes opened up to a reality that I did not appreciate.

Many years later, now as a D&I practitioner, I was asked to write for *Diversity Journal* in the US, to bring in an international point of view, which led me to write about diversity around the world, a look at challenges and practices in various countries.

Diversity Around the World

(Published in Diversity Journal 2 December 2011) When we talk about *diversity* we often think about the USA. Why? Because this is where you find most books, networks and magazines about the subject. And legislation around diversity, or rather discrimination, came in to place as early (or as late, depending on you point of view) as 1961. But diversity is everywhere and it is a subject in many regions and countries, but the focus may be different, the laws may be different, and the understanding of what *diversity* is may be different.

When reading about legislative requirements on diversity in various countries, there seems to be one group that has prominence in most countries; people with disabilities. In large regions and countries like Canada, India and Europe, there is also attention around hiring and promoting women. Norway even has a quota of 40% women on boards for public limited companies. But from there on, which minorities receive the most attention varies like the world itself. In many places there is no legal ruling, but there may (or may not) be an expectation - sort of an unwritten rule - of hiring minorities in both the public and private sectors. There are also different opinions on whether there should be a legal ruling or not.

To give you an idea, I am inviting you on a brief journey around the world. Below you will find a selection of countries that have laws around promoting diversity and/or disadvantaged groups in their populations - other than women and people with disabilities (acknowledging that there may be more legislative requirements I have not come across in my search):

- *Brazil:* Black and native Brazilians
- *Canada:* People of Aboriginal descent, visible minorities
- *France:* Obligation to accept a certain number of students in from poor families (often of North-African descent)
- *India:* Scheduled Castes (Dalit or 'untouchables') and Tribes (two groupings of historically disadvantaged people); other underserved classes ("socially and educationally backward classes")
- *Malaysia:* Bumiputra (ethnic Malay). This affirmative action is by some named as discriminatory and by others as a means to defuse inter-ethnic tension.
- *New Zealand:* People of Maori and Polynesian descent
- *People's Republic of China:* Certain public positions are distributed to ethnic minorities (non-Han people)
- *South Africa:* Blacks, Indians and people of colour
- *United Kingdom:* Catholics/Protestants

In several countries in the Middle East, there are laws around hiring more *local* staff (e.g. Qatarization), as the oil industry has brought in large numbers of expatriates.

I don't think there is a country that has it all figured out, but I would like to highlight Singapore as a nation that is rather successful in mixing minority/majority groups and religions. Most Singaporeans are of Chinese, Malay or Indian descent. There are four official languages: English, Chinese, Malay and Tamil. Within this little space (694 sq km/268 sq mi) people practice Buddhism, Christianity, Islam, Taoism and Hinduism. They celebrate all the various religious/festive days and show a respect for each other that is rather unique. Not that there's no tension or discrimination, but generally speaking it is a peaceful nation that has embraced its diversity. Alas, these are best practice examples.

Why do we need laws to promote recruitment or student intake of certain groups in the first place? This is a big question, but we seem to have a tendency to create in- and out-groups, on micro and macro levels, and you find it everywhere around the globe to varying degrees. I will not go into the psychological reasons as to why we have this tendency, but the good news is that as humans we adapt and we learn. The fact that so many countries have legislation around diversity, is already a step forward, it means we are aware of the unbalance. Progress may not be at revolutionary speed, but we are coming to an understanding that diversity makes business-sense and that the diversity of the world is at our doorsteps.

Simply said, achieving diversity and respect for people is a challenge all over the world, but there is also good progress going on around the world.

*

Next follows a blog I wrote about the wish for *uniformity*; that we seem to resist anything that is different, or people that are different from ourselves. There are several questions asked of the reader: "What if..?" and it is meant to make you reflect next time you move into judging other people's choices. And the word *judging* is not meant negatively, for it is a matter of fact that we do it all the time. Being aware that we judge usually opens us up to other perspectives and angles. Here I would also like to mention that related to judging other people's behaviour, we also do a lot of *assuming* something about others. We might not have all data, so we guess. The guessing tends to come out negatively about the other person, but not always, or we use our own frame of what is right or wrong, good or bad. As for judging, being aware that we also assume, often creates the possibility in our mind that the there are other solutions, or other realities.

Diversity or Differences in Daily Life

There are many good reasons why a company should be diverse and inclusive; plainly speaking because it affects the bottom line (numbers to be found in *final remarks* at the end of the chapter). Summarized in few words:

1 - A diverse employee group represents and therefore understands the external world = company produces the products the customers want and need.

2 - A diverse environment where people feel included, whether they are gay, have an impairment, green hair, or generally have different ideas/backgrounds from others = productive, engaged staff who are loyal and give their best at work.

Many companies get this and work towards it. But what about people in general? Outside of work? Do *we* get it? Do we understand the benefits of diversity, or differences, in our society?

National cultures, corporate cultures, educational cultures, religious cultures, and social levels (the list could be longer) have certain codes and expectations around how we should live our lives. And on top of that, I think many feel a need to create uniformity; people should be the same, because it is something we can understand and connect with, and it feels safe. When people do something out of the box, we may feel confused, puzzled or even slightly envious.

For example, a colleague of mine shared that in her home country and in her family culture it is common to take several degrees at university. My colleague wanted to concentrate on one degree and felt it was a good choice. The others couldn't understand it, "you should take two, at least", and they made her feel that she had made a bad decision. She didn't do what the others did, she stood out from the family crowd, and many years later she still feels like the black sheep when being with her family. Most places people would feel good about having accomplished to get any kind of degree, and here we have this person feeling bad about having just *one*!

It makes me think; what if everyone wanted to (and could) be scientists? Who would pick up the garbage then? Or if everyone wanted to work at the supermarket, who would invent Iphones or the internet? Our diversity of interests, skills, competencies, talents, the choices we make, our opinions, this is what makes the world go round. Do we appreciate that?

My colleague was an example of an educational expectation, but there are so many other assumptions from the culture we belong to. The expectation of *uniformity* could involve getting married, having children, house, car, income level, charity, contribution in family, even expectations around how to behave according to your gender. What is the worst-case result if we give in to all these expectations? We would be the same! (That would be terribly boring) And not only that, people lose energy, creativity, and joy if they have to pretend to be someone they are not.

We need diversity, we *need* differences in daily life. It is such a banal and simple truth, yet I think we need to remind ourselves of it regularly. Curiosity and an open mind are good starting points when meeting people who are 'different' (whatever that means to you).

As we become more and more exposed to differences from other countries, we might also feel threatened by all the differences that some people feel are forced upon us. Talking with Samira Abbadi, Dutch national born of Moroccan parents, she told me about being from a minority culture in The Netherlands. She is weary of the negative flow of energy regarding immigration in Europe these days, and the fear of terrorism. She wants to influence, e.g. through social media, a new focus on the positive aspects of a mixed global world. Samira works as a Program Director at De Baak Institute for Leadership, Entrepreneurship and Personal Development.

"I would like to share an example on how diversity inspires entrepreneurship. You might have heard of the main square and open-air theatre Djemaa El-Fna in Marrakesh. It's a magical place where people come to eat, to meet, to listen to music, to be entertained.

"A Dutch national thought of copying this concept in The Netherlands, more specifically Rotterdam, a city with many diverse cultures and nationalities. The idea was to make an event out of it; a possibility for traders, artists and musicians to come together in one place.

"The first time the event was held in Rotterdam was in September 2013 and it attracted 12,000 visitors, the next year 15,000 visitors (I am looking forward to being part of the organization in autumn 2015). The participants were Dutch, Moroccans, Spanish, Chinese - and many other minorities living in Rotterdam. The event attracted people from all social levels and people of all ages, and it is now considered to be an inspiration to entrepreneurship and craftsmanship. There was such a variety of things to see, do (storytelling, poetry, having your hands painted with henna) and eat. I'm a food lover myself, and I loved the way people invented new dishes; like mixing traditional Moroccan and Dutch food. Being part of this event makes me feel proud and 'twice at home'; in both Morocco and in The Netherlands.

"These days there is a lot of negativity around immigration and people of different religions living together. Reading the newspapers can be depressing. But if you look around where you live, you might notice that people of different nationalities and faiths are mixing and that there is a lot of variety offered in your city because of the additional nationalities; e.g. dance and food. For me the example of Djemaa El-Fna in Rotterdam shows how we can create something positive from new ideas and diverse backgrounds. We embrace diversity, without politics. I think it brings new perspectives, which is useful for life and good for work.

"My parents taught me to be an ambassador of my origins, to be proud of my roots. I openly share Moroccan traditions and I try to show that Muslim people are like everyone else. It does take courage, though - a lot of people in The Netherlands are tired of diversity, maybe because of an over-exposure in the media. But I was raised to be generous - I focus on the positive, without being superficial or being too explicit. By that I mean I want to contribute to a better society in the country I live: "I am diversity"."

There is a link to the Rotterdam event (including a map) - in Dutch - in the reference list.

Final Remarks

"Diversity: the art of thinking independently together."
- Malcolm Forbes

As I am sure you know and have experienced, mixing different people together can be challenging. Misunderstandings often happen when you have different languages, values, and customs in one place. This easily raises the tension between people. But... challenges are also opportunities; tension can inspire something new.

Every year there is some report (e.g. Forbes' study, McKinsey; Diversity Matters, Harvard Business School articles) that proves the business sense of having a diverse and inclusive business. Having *evidence and data* is not the challenge. Still, to underline the fact, I'd like to close out this short chapter on general diversity by sharing some numbers that stood out to me in a report from the *Financial Times*.

For those who would like to dive further into the business case, I can recommend the book *Diversity at Work. The Business Case for Equity* by Trevor Wilson and the McKinsey report from 2015 *Diversity Matters*.

The *Financial Times'* report on 'The Inclusive Workplace' May 2014: "Research last year by the New York-based Center for Talent Innovation (CTI), (…), began to take us a step closer. Involving more than 40 case studies and 1,800 employee surveys, it looked at what it termed *two-dimensional diversity,* namely *inherent diversity* - such as gender and race - combined with *acquired diversity* - such as global experience and language skills. "It found that publicly-traded companies with two-dimensional diversity were 45 per cent more likely than those without to have expanded market share in the past year and 70 per cent more likely to have captured a new market. When teams had one or more members who represented a target end-user, the entire team was as much as 158 per cent more likely to understand that target end-user and innovate accordingly.

"CTI has also found that 77 percent of women want to invest in companies with diverse leadership teams."

From the same report: "An experiment by Massachusetts-based_Tufts University demonstrated that diverse _groups perform better than homogeneous_teams by when it deployed 200 people in_mock juries - the mixed juries all performed better than those comprising only white or only black jurors. Groupthink may lead to a cohesive team, but one that will happily agree on the same costly mistake."

What about you? Where do you see the benefits of diversity in your surroundings?

(Talking about surroundings, my life wouldn't have been the same without Indian restaurants, the kebab place with great falafels, the food market where I can get real spicy stuff and exotic ingredients.)

CHAPTER FOUR:
ZOOMING IN ON NATIONAL CULTURE

What is 'culture'? There are many cultures: professional, corporate, educational, national (and geographical within a nation), religious/spiritual, sexual orientation, generational, family, and gender. All of these cultures influence us-we see the world through our cultural lens(es). Another important point is that we *learn* culture and cultural language - it is not inherited.

How does culture influence us?

- o The way we interact with other people, including various communication styles
- o How we conduct work
- o Our behavior and style
- o Our use of language
- o How we solve challenges, problems, and conflicts
- o How we negotiate
- o How we go about creating relationships.

In this chapter I will talk about *national* culture, which means the culture of our country of origin. Some of us have indeed several national cultures in one, for example if you were born in the UK to Pakistani parents, you would grow up with two national cultures and be coloured by both. Some would even say that they live in a third culture; children of parents with different nationalities who have grown up in a country non-native to their parents or they might have lived around the world. These children often feel most *at home* culturally with other *third culture kids* - often named 'TCK's'.

National culture remains one of my favourite interests. I did my first overseas travel at the age of 17, without my parents (they were not happy about it). I was away for about two months, traveling around the USA, and I discovered a new world. The most exciting was staying with a family that was neighbour to and accepted by the Amish people in Indiana. This lovely family, with whom I still keep in touch, gave me the task to take care of their horses. I still vividly see the eyes of the Amish children when I rode by, sitting on the horse without a saddle, a young European woman with short hair. They looked at me like I was from another planet! And I thought they looked quite exotic myself!

Now working as a consultant, giving workshops and training sessions on cross-cultural communication and cross-cultural intelligence, I have become very aware of the national culture filters we humans use to judge others and ourselves - which often leads to a feeling of better than/less than others. That includes myself. I still make unintentional mistakes, which I learn from; I still use my Norwegian filter or experiences - although now I am able to discover my mistakes half-way through or after the situation. At least, so I think! The interesting and humbling part about working in this field, is that I never feel like I will ever finish learning.

And learning isn't always about the *other culture*; it is also about my own. When you are within the culture you grew up with, it can be hard to see others from the outside. As I have been moving in and out of my own (Norwegian) culture, I find it fascinating to see Norwegians from the inside and outside. One one occasion, while I was conducting a workshop for the European Women's Professional Network (EPWN, now PWN) in Norway, I had a wonderful opportunity to hear from several nationalities about their experience of Norway. The workshop was on "Living and Working in Norway. How to Maximise Communication and Relationships". There were women from Japan, China, Gran Canarias, UK, France, New Zealand, Serbia, Philippines, Finland and the USA: Women who had lived in Norway from one month to fifteen years, so quite a diversity in the Norwegian cultural experience.

It was an amazing group. Their honesty and willingness to share their experiences helped everyone in the room. With their different cultural backgrounds, each had different experiences of what it was like to live in Norway and interact with Norwegians. Personally, I got a lot out of what they described. It made me remember that yes, we are definitely coloured by our national culture and yes, we are individuals that may have little in common with the generalized type. I have often *said* that "generalisations are helpful, but don't forget the individual differences". After this encounter, I *felt* it even more strongly.

Within generalisations there are so many nuances. Example: an American lady said that people look at her like she's mad if she talks with them at the bus stop. It is true that Norwegians are shy and would not normally do that. And yet, I and some others do... When I was in Norway once a lady on a train started talking to me because my handbag looked like an animal of some sort (a bear?). The nuance is to see the signals: Do they look back at you and smile? Does their body language indicate an openness to talking? These nuances are hard to see when you are new in a culture, but practice makes you a master!

Having moved countries several times, I know that it is hard to acquire new friends and acquaintances when you're a stranger, and that's a fact in many countries, not only Norway (which some self-bashers in a seminar I attended seemed to think). Going in and out of my own culture I can see my home country with new eyes, again and again - it is a great learning experience.

The realisations about my own culturally-tinted glasses and filters, inspired me to write the following two blogs about values:

Cultural Values

Values and beliefs are learned within a national culture, and they may be largely subconscious. You may not be aware of your own values and beliefs until you are confronted with someone who is different to you. Values vary enormously, especially across national cultures. We have a tendency to judge others' behaviour based on our own cultural norms, the 'lens' we see through. This creates lots of opportunities for potential conflict, misunderstandings, and miscommunication. Different values lead to different behaviour, behavior you may not understand. It is important that we try to learn and appreciate these differences in order to work effectively with people from other cultures. A team with a variety of values might experience some misunderstandings at first, but they will most likely also experience more creativity when values are understood and appreciated.

I remember an example from 2001 - 2004 when I worked in a European department. Many of the lead positions were located in the UK, and by default many of the managers in international roles were British. The Brits value politeness, and one way of expressing this is through indirect communication. The challenge in this European setting was that the non-Brits did not understand the Brits' long sentences and their indirect way of telling what they wanted done - which often ended up in confusion or even no action at all. The UK managers also gave feedback to their subordinates in other countries that they should be more polite, which didn't mean the same in another local setting, where direct communication was the norm. The intent was good, but the feedback was not always understood or well taken - therefore producing unintended consequences. We tend to transfer our own values, and the behaviour that goes with it, onto others - mostly unconsciously - and this could unintentionally harm the relationship.

Speaking of the quality of *politeness*. I find both the British and Americans to be generally polite people. But not in all situations... Have you ever taken a local train in London during rush hour? Or driven a car in Houston, Texas? *Polite* wouldn't be the description that comes to mind!

Or what about the value of *good service*? I commuted between the US and the Netherlands for work some years ago, and noticed a big difference in what *good service* means. Entering a shop in the US, shopworkers would be very attentive and smiling, but often had a lack of knowledge of the product, so that if I asked questions - they needed to get the supervisor. In the Netherlands, I noticed rather the opposite; deep knowledge about the product, but very little greeting and smiling. Yet both nationalities were behaving according to what is considered *good service*.

Working with various nationalities, I have seen myself and colleagues change, when we get information about the values of the other culture. It is like there is a 'light bulb moment'. We then understand the behaviour and develop more patience for the other person. It doesn't mean that everything runs smoothly all of a sudden, but it sure helps!

Individual versus Group Values

According to Trompenaars and Hampden-Turner, who have done research on culture and cultural differences and who I tend to refer to as *cultural gurus*, individuals are either self-or community-oriented. Which community/group we identify with differs enormously, e.g. the French tend to identify with country and family, the Japanese with the corporation, and the Irish with the Roman Catholic Church.

If one compares societies, taking the examples of the US and China, I agree that you could label the Americans self-oriented and the Chinese community/group-focused. But, at an individual level we are more complex than that, and I believe we have a mix of individiual and group values.

But what *is* a group value within a group? I worked in a job which involved collaborating with several European teams in which the *team group value* seemed to be steered by the dominating culture, which was a forced-onto value; or a top-down approach. It can be experienced as if you are obligated to behave in a certain way, and it does not produce a productive team feeling. Successful international teams discuss values and agree on which ones the team wants to make their own.

While our individual/personal values are unlikely to change in a group, it is however likely that we *adapt our behaviours* to fit in with the group. This does not always happen, but it probably occurs more often than you think. You can still stay authentic to yourself, at the same time as trying to understand the other and accommodate your behaviour to create a win-win situation for both of you. This is behaving in a 'culturally intelligent' way.

Taking the discussion a bit further, it has been argued that individualism is the trend of modern society, but is it really? How often does someone invent a new product all on his or her own? Or how often do we achieve something only out of our own efforts - with no help from friends, partners or family?

National Identity, the Feeling of "Me"

Life can be confusing when you keep moving around. A coach asked me; "So, tell me about yourself, who are you?" I answered: "It depends on the circumstances and which country I'm in!" Well, that's a slight exaggeration, but there is some truth to it. As I have moved around the world and worked in international jobs, I have noticed that my feeling of identity - who I am relative to others - changes slightly according to the circumstances.

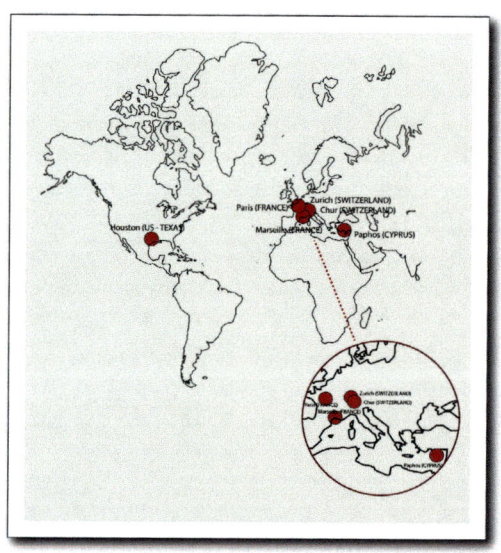

I went to study in Switzerland when I was 20 years old. I was in an international student environment and only really made Swiss friends when I had a work placement in a local company, and in the last semester at school. I remember comparing the Swiss culture to the Norwegian, and noticed a big difference regarding humour. What made the Swiss laugh didn't make me laugh. I was amazed at the dislike of *others*. People in the German canton (county) didn't like the people in the French or Italian canton, and vice versa. Even between villages there could be negative feelings. There weren't fond feelings for the Germans from Germany either. Most Swiss people could not place my accent and often thought I was German - which at times led to bad service or just a negative attitude towards me. This is my general impression and it is a generalization: there are of course many Swiss people who like those from their neighbouring villages, cantons, and countries. Nevertheless, I was rather puzzled by this general dislike of *others* and I couldn't see any advantages of this attitude in today's world. What I admired, though, was the value *respect for nature*. They were very advanced regarding recycling and day-to-day behaviour like bringing your own shopping bag and not throwing plastic into the wild environment. The Norwegians have the same value, but they were not as advanced as the Swiss back then. Through my time in Switzerland, 3.5 years in all, I kept a Norwegian identity and kept comparing Switzerland to Norway.

An additional experience in Switzerland was comparing Norwegian women with the upper middle-class Asian women who were fellow students. One girl from Singapore said honestly that she was in Switzerland to find a rich husband, another girl from Sri Lanka had found a husband, but was disappointed to realize that he was not rich after all - having had an image that everyone in Switzerland would be so. I felt very fortunate that as a Norwegian girl I didn't need to marry at all if I didn't feel like it.

At the age of 23 I moved to Cyprus to work in a five-star hotel in the town of Paphos, in the west of the island. Due to my Swiss education, I moved straight into the management team, quite a treat for such a young person! And this is when I noticed a huge difference in culture: I thought the hotel vice-director was an idiot for screaming at me in front of hotel guests, but he only wanted to show he was a strong manager. It took me a while to understand why most of the staff seemed so happy to see me. I treated them as equals, something they were not used to from a member of the management team. This is also when I started realizing that other 'rules' can work as well as the rules I had grown up with. For example, in traffic, the bigger car had the right to go first. In a crossroad, you stop for the truck, it's just logical! I noticed that women had more limitations on what was considered good behaviour than what men did, but felt I was given more space, as I was a foreigner. There was also a general attitude of 'I help you now, you help me later', which I found quite pleasant and also practical. I started to adapt and did a little less comparison of the two cultures. Though I always felt like a foreigner, it didn't feel negative like it had in Switzerland, maybe due to the fact that the Cypriots are a very welcoming people. However, I was not always proud to say I was Norwegian, as my fellow countrymen and - women did not show their best sides on holiday on the east side of the island. So, with these factors present, my identity felt different from before. I was more of a 'mix'.

Then… moving back to Norway. I had a repatriation shock after a good five years abroad. I came back the year when the winter Olympics was hosted by Norway (1994), and patriotism was at an all-time high! I felt embarrassed to be Norwegian; I thought they were full of themselves! And an identity of *being European* had started to develop - I had seen other ways of being and living, I felt connected to other cultures as well.

I moved from the hotel industry to recruitment, and then to human resources (HR) - I started working in a large international company, where I stayed for ten years, in various international roles, working from Norway, the US and France. Most of the time I was the only Norwegian in teams and departments, and also the only Scandinavian. My egalitarian attitude was a blessing and a curse; mostly welcomed, but some times a disadvantage, not all superiors were comfortable with it. I adjusted as best as I could, by using more indirect language and involving my manager in more details, but egalitarianism being such an ingrained value and 'under my skin', I think people still felt it no matter how hard I tried to downplay my 'equal standing'. I'm not saying that having an egalitarian attitude is wrong or bad, but when a direct line manager feels threatened by you it is a challenge for the working relationship. The time I worked in international roles from Norway my feeling of identiy was quite mixed. I felt European when I was physically in Norway, but felt European-Norwegian when I was abroad working with mixed nationality teams.

At the age of 35, I packed my bags again, this time for Houston, Texas! Visiting the villages (locals might call them small towns) around Texas, I loved seeing that people actually *do* wear cowboy boots and stetsons! Very exotic! Regarding building relationships, I did misunderstand now and then, even if I had been exposed to the American culture a few times before. When people said; "we should meet for lunch or dinner", I actually believed they meant it! And I don't think I really grasped the underlying racial tensions, nor the American culture's view on making friends. At my work place there were not many African-American managers or consultants, and in hindsight I think some of the African-American secretaries didn't know how/where to place me. I had the same egalitarian attitude as always, but the way they disappeared on me when I left my job, I must have misunderstood what I thought was a friendship. I was hurt, but later on I got an *aha!* moment while reading *Riding the Waves of Culture* by Trompenaars and Hampden-Turner, and learned about *Lewin's circles*. The Americans have much larger public specs than Europeans do - and therefore share more of their private lives at work. Doing that in Europe means that you are becoming friends - so I thought we were friends. I was also a *white manager*, and although that didn't mean anything to me, it probably did to others. Ignorance is bliss... (*and* a disadvantage..)

You might notice that I talk about *Europe* again and not my home country Norway. And that was my identity when I lived in the US - I felt European. I identified with the long-term thinking and historical roots of the European.

The stay in the US became shorter than planned. My husband-to-be was asked to return to Europe, and I had realised that I needed to change direction; from HR to Diversity & Inclusion. That's where I felt passion and engagement while working. So, my next country was France, the home country of my husband. And not only France, but Mediterranean France. Boom - culture shock! From a 'yes-we-can' country' to a 'no-that's-not-possible' country. From a relatively egalitarian culture to a relatively macho one. And this is where I went back to feeling very Norwegian. The values were too different from my own, it was not comfortable. My personal and national values are equality and honesty and I was suddenly confronted with: women taking a more traditional role and being objectified, hierarchy at work and in private life, and for the first time I was among people thinking it was okay to buy goods that 'fell off the truck'. I had never felt more Norwegian in my life! The circle was complete.

My own take-away from these experiences is that I find it interesting to see how one's national identity might change as circumstances change. And not only that, people label you differently. By moving to southern France I had all of a sudden become *tall, blond and introvert* - in the eyes of the locals. In Norway I was used to the idea of being j*ust under average height*, having *red-brown hair* and being *extravert*...

Both the internal and the external processes can feel rather confusing when living abroad for many years; *Who am I? And How am I compared to other people?* Additionally, it is quite common to take on parts of the culture and practices of the countries you have lived in - you actually become a mix after a while. This is something I get reminded of whenever I go back to Norway for holidays and work (examples follow in a blog called *Adapting to a culture, does it mean forgetting your own?*).

Successful Cross-Cultural Teams

Moving now from the personal side of things to the work-related topic of being involved in international teams... In my exprience, there is no 'one size fits all' on this subject. Creating an environment of trust when people from different national cultures are working together, requires making an effort to build a common understanding, along with trust and commitment.

This takes time, and it is a *team* obligation. Personally, I find that I can quite quickly orient myself by making certain observations:

- o Is this person task- or relationship-oriented? Can I send an email with the tasks I would like help on, or do I need to build a relationship first?
- o Does she or he come from a high-trust or a low-trust society? There are differences in how easily people build trust with someone, e.g. in high-trust countries like Denmark, Japan and Germany, you need less time to 'prove' yourself than in low-trust countries like France, China and Mexico.
- o What about sharing information? Is that done willingly or otherwise?
- o What is *clear instruction* in a direct communication country versus an indirect communication country?

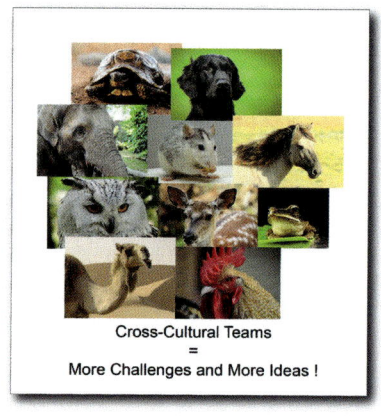

Cross-Cultural Teams
=
More Challenges and More Ideas !

In most cases, people around the world appreciate you being interested in them. Be curious: ask your staff/colleagues about their cultural background. You can also read up on the country and/or talk with others of the same nationality. I find it useful to connect with what is important to people, what is below the surface of the person's 'iceberg', the part you cannot see, and with their inner core values and beliefs. Some questions that might come in handy are:

- o In your country, what is the accepted role of education? Do you agree with this?
- o What does *family* mean to you?
- o I would be interested in learning what values are strong in your country, can you tell me about them ? (You can give your own

example first, like "In my country we have a lot of respect for nature and you can see that in people's behaviour, e.g recycling, picking up glass in the forest, etc.")

Building trust and commitment across cultures mean that you need to use all parts of your cultural intelligence: intercultural engagement (motivation, attitude), cultural understanding (knowing yourself, knowing the other), and intercultural communication (verbal, non-verbal, communication styles). Listen, be emphatic, speak to people's hearts and minds, 'lean in', be respectful - and you will build trust and be trusted.

The current *virtuality* does add some complexities, but also *flexibility*. I've been in some discussions where people say "I still prefer to see my colleague in the office, I still prefer to have a coach in front of me". We are social beings; some more, some less. Some training is best done face-to-face, while some training is best done individually and at their own speed. Meeting people on the phone and through video is effective and saves time, but in conflict situations you are more likely to solve the issue quicker if you can get together. Meeting in person or via video allows you to see the body language (but on video you can't touch), while meeting over the phone allows you to really hear the person - both versions are effective.

Virtuality presents more options and flexibility, but it doesn't take away the need to meet other people in flesh and blood sometimes.

The complexities apart, creating some common ground rules does help building trust and commitment. And even better, make sure you talk with team members about what those ground rules really mean to them.

*

Having myself felt strongly misjudged because of cultural differences and spoken with others who felt the same, I wrote the following blog about giving feedback across cultures:

Giving Feedback; What Lenses do you Wear?

Most of us receive feedback of some sort - from bosses and colleagues, in training, from friends and relatives, from neighbours - in short, from a range of different people. Some feedback feels really good, like compliments about work well done. It may feel embarrassing there and then, depending on how you perceive compliments and your cultural upbringing. But even if you feel embarrassed, at one point it will feel good. Then there is feedback about changes you should make; some can feel fair and you think that this is very good advice. And then there are the ones that make you feel bad. You may feel shocked, angry, hurt, unfairly treated, stepped over, misunderstood, etc., etc. And you have a choice: should you consider this feedback even if it is painful or it feels wrong, or should you throw it away?

"All feedback is a gift, take it or leave it" is a phrase I have heard often, and I use it myself. But, still... saying it this way leaves all the responsibility on the receiver. Doesn't the giver have some responsibility too? I would say yes. Because we tend to judge according to our preferences, our cultural values, our style, our tastes, our standards - in fact we judge from the view our own lenses. When we give feedback it says something about ourselves: our preferences, what we think is right or wrong. Being aware that our version of the world might not be the same, shows respect for the other.

Example One: Someone with extravert behaviours and preferences thinks her team members are introverts - and she tells them so (wanting the outcome that they change). The team conducts a team evaluation and one of the results shows that the woman mentioned comes out at the extreme end of being extravert. Her team members are also extraverts, but not as much as she is. She gave them feedback as seen from her extreme end, not being able to see the nuances and range of being extravert.

Example Two: A supervisor gives feedback to an employee that he is too blunt/too direct and that he needs to change the way he communicates with people. The supervisor comes from a culture where indirect communication is valued and the employee comes from a culture where direct communication is the norm. The employee works in a direct culture, therefore in this case the supervisor is judging from his own values rather than seeing the environment the employee operates in.

In both cases above, the feedback-giver failed to review and get a holistic view of the situation before making judgment. So how can we make sure we give inclusive feedback? I think the main thing is to look at a situation from different perspectives, and to take a bird's eye view. Creating a dialogue is important, a space where the receiver feels both listened to and seen, that she or he feels you have the best intentions, and that you are both OPEN to different perspectives. I believe that is when change can and will happen, and that it creates a win-win situation.

Next time you give or receive feedback, be curious, think about the lenses that you have on, the perspective you are coming from ... "Am I giving this feedback out of positive intent and wanting to help, or am I just annoyed that she or he is not *doing it my way*? And if you are at the receiving end, you do have a choice whether you take it on board or not, considering your own cultural lens ... "Would it be useful for me to adapt my behaviour to achieve a better result in this situation or in this relationship? " ... The answer could be yes, could be no, but either way you are being conscious of your choice.

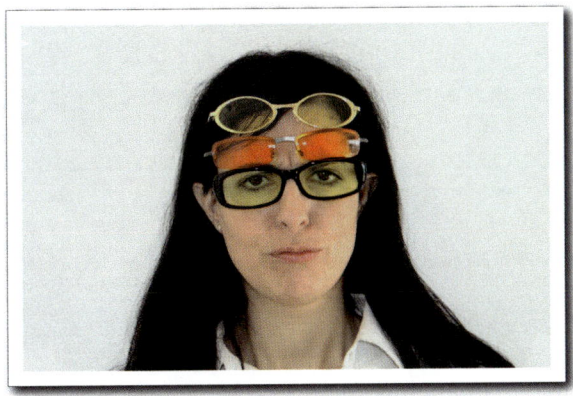

*

I have often heard the French apologise for their bad English, and it is true that many French have a strong accent. They are not exposed to other languages since all movies and programmes are dubbed. There is also a big French music market. They rarely hear another language and it is therefore understandable that they have a strong accent. Having worked in international roles for 15 years now, I have learned to appreciate that the most important elements of good communication across cultures are willingness to communicate and to try to understand. The accent isn't that important as long as you can get your message through. The given is a medium mastery level of the common language - in many cases English.

The article that follows, published in *Diversity Journal* December 7, 2012, was inspired by some workshops and trainings I gave in which the English language was mentioned as a challenge.

Language: What is Efficient Communication?

In my role as an international coach/trainer/consultant I have come across several people who have questions when it comes to communicating in another language: Will I be able to explain to my mentor what I really mean? How can I be sure that my sub-contractor in country X understands me? Will I be able to transmit the training content in what is now my fourth language? What language level can I expect from my foreign staff?

These are all very relevant questions in our globalized world. We want to say what we mean, and we want others to receive what we send-which can be hard enough even when we share the same mother tongue.

It is good that we strive to communicate effectively, and at an advanced level when speaking a foreign language. But these days I find that we often need to be pragmatic and instead strive for 'what is good enough'. Which brings me to another question: how do we know *what* is good enough?

A good start would be to consider the following two key questions;

o Did I express myself clearly enough? (Even if it took longer than desired)
o Did the receiver get the message that I wanted to transmit? (You could check by, for example, asking the other to repeat what you said)

Getting a *yes* to both, communication should in principal be good enough, whether it is oral or written. If you get *no* or *maybe*, ask yourself what you could have done differently. And if you manage someone who is trying to learn your language, you can ask these questions to your employee to help him/her progress.

For those who speak multiple languages, if you convey uncertainty, that is what will be received. If you talk with confidence, even knowing you make lots of mistakes, the receiver will look beyond your flaws and listen to the message you are giving. I have seen people deliver speeches in poor English, but with such charm and ease that a strong accent, mistakes, asking people for help to find words, and strange translations only added color and fun to the presentation.

And what if you have an accent? It likely will never go away, so embrace it as part of your personality! Some people do succeed in copying the accent of the language they are learning, which is a good goal, but not necessary. The main objective is to have people understand you, not to sound exactly like them.

For those of you lucky enough to have English as your mother tongue, I would recommend starting to learn another language. When traveling you will likely connect with people at another level, you get great brain exercise, and you will probably start communicating more efficiently with all those foreigners who are trying hard to master *your* language. You will find yourself understanding their creative explanations when you have had to be creative in another language yourself.

Effective communication in a foreign language should include the receiver and sender understanding the same thing, with willingness from both sides to be creative and open - and a little humor doesn't hurt, either.

Bonne chance! Good luck! Lykke til! Viel Glück!

*

When working with one or several other cultures, we sometimes need to slightly adapt to the other in order to make things work smoothly, and simultaneously stay authentic to ourselves. But, that is easier said than done, and how much should one adapt, whether you are an expat, an immigrant, or working in an international company? These were questions that made me write the following blog.

Adapting to a Culture, Does it Mean Forgetting Your Own?

We talk a lot about *successful integration* in Europe, mostly in the terms of how much immigrants take on traditions and rules of their new home country. Or rather how *unsuccessful* the integration is... There's a lot of fear from ethnic Europeans around non-western immigrants creating their own ghettos, a place where they keep entirely to their own language and customs. After 9/11 in the US and terrorist attacks in Europe, that fear has increased. And then there is the fear within the immigrants themselves, that they will adapt too much to their new home country, forgetting about their original traditions and values.

I am not sure I am comfortable with the word *integration*... Let me introduce another term, or question: what is *successful adaptation*? I would imagine that it is a state of mind where you have assimilated the customs and rules of your new country, yet you keep values which are important to you.

CULTURE AND DIVERSITY

You may have heard about the *expatriate morale curve*. It describes how it is normal to feel ups and downs in stages of adaptation during a stay abroad, and I would say that these ups and downs keep coming, even when you have emigrated and know that the country you have settled in is your new home country. Some unfamiliar habits are easy to adapt to, others less so and still others you may not want at all.

I am an immigrant myself - from northern Europe to southern. It is not as dramatic a change as moving from Asia to Europe, but there are quite a few differences. For example, I had to learn the language (not easy!), the code of politeness, rules, law (in my case for business), eat at different times and in a certain order and with several dishes, understand women's role in society, communication style, status and hierarchy, and so on and so on: the list is long. Certain things I have adapted to, for example showing anger is okay, or not following all the rules as much as we do in northern Europe (it is quite practical to park illegally for five minutes and put your warning sign when you just need to deliver something quickly). But I don't think I will ever agree with all the big and small differences of women in society compared to my origins (e.g. to be quiet when people are referring to my husband's house or car - it is OUR house and car!). Because it touches my values. And I have started forgetting some cultural habits. An example is a business meeting I had in Norway. I had forgotten that in Norway we jump straight to the point, without too much small-talk to 'warm up'. So I tried to build a relationship first, which wasn't necessary at all!

So adapting ... Is it a threat to you? Will you forget your origins? Yes, you will probably adapt over time, which could mean forgetting some cultural codes and habits. This is in fact practical and it makes sense. It is *survival of the fittest* - we humans have historically been masters at adapting to our environments. But I do not think we *forget* our values, as they are too deeply rooted. Which takes me to a tricky question... What if our values do not fit with the new home country values? What do we do then?

*

Slightly on the same subject, the following blog came about due to a training session I created for a Norwegian public organisation. When preparing for the session, I started asking myself questions. What is the difference between immigrant challenges and advantages, and working across cultures in an international company?

Immigration versus Cross-culture

Together with a local business partner I delivered a training in Norway that we called *The Strength of Multi-Cultural Competence*. She (an American in Norway) brought the local facts and research and I (a Norwegian in France) brought the general theory and international research. As I read up on the immigration statistics and handbooks for successful encounters with immigrants from the Norwegian government, I wondered whether I was the right woman for the job. Maybe they should have had an expert on immigration instead? At the same time, I thought the combination of my partner's experience and mine would together produce an enriching learning opportunity for the participants. And as the training went by, with feedback from the participants, I got a stronger feeling for the differences and similarities between talking about *immigration* and talking about *cross-culture*. Or rather cross-cultural communication in a country versus cross-cultural communication in a company.

What is similar?
- The need for *intercultural intelligence*. According to the interculturalist Elisabeth Plum (*Cultural Intelligence; the art of leading cultural complexity*), we need to be motivated to interact effectively with someone from a different national culture, we need to have knowledge about our own and the other's culture, and finally to switch off the 'auto pilot' and intelligently combine motivation and knowledge with various verbal and non-verbal communication tools.
- The importance of getting more information and assume positive intent.
- Being aware of stereotypes, prejudices and unconscious biases.
- That we have the tendency to recruit and promote those that are

similar to us.

What is different?
- The discussion around *they* (the immigrants) have entered our arena, in other words "why should WE change?" This may also be present in a global company in various forms, but I would still say that there is a slightly stronger sense of *us versus them* when talking about immigration, and a stronger hold on traditions and behaviours from the majority national culture. It is likely that in a given company culture there would be some discussion around who should change/adapt, but my experience is that people are slightly more open to change to fit in (typically the headquarter culture sets the overall culture, but it is not necessarily so).
- Awareness around changing population demographics and the impact it has on the country (more diversity!).

My conclusion is: there are more similarities than differences between the related topics. Which makes me think that interculturalists and immigration experts can indeed swap ideas and research. Do they do that today? No idea. When I look at online discussions (e.g. LinkedIn) I get the impression that the interculturalists talk with each other, the linguistic experts talk with each other, and then there is a separate discussion altogether from, for example, the EU Commission on diversity dialogues. But, this is an impression only, I have not conducted any formal research on it.

*

Talking about immigration, Bart Romanow, a Polish Executive Development Adviser living in Norway, has some stories about meeting the Norwegian culture; he calls them *Norwegian adventures*.

"Some months ago my company was to deliver a tender. One of the required attachments was the confirmation that the company was not found guilty of criminal offences. Norway is a very digitalized country. A physical person can apply for such a certificate using an electronic signature, via an official Police website. For companies, you have to print, fill in and send the form by snail mail (this is somehow strange in the context that almost 100% of all forms and public administration related procedures for companies is organised digitally, but this seemed still to be a clear formality.)

"After around two weeks I called this Police department to check when we would get the certificate. A nice lady on the other side of the phone line managed to find our application quite fast. She said that they have so many applications coming in, that our application was still waiting in the long queue. I was surprised, as this was not in the middle of July... when things like this might happen in Norway. I remember this was on Thursday. And here comes the other surprise. On Monday morning we got an email from one of the Police department officers. Saying; "Hei Harald, politiattest utsendes i dag." Translation: A Policeman was informing us with an email, using my boss' first name (by the way, they have never met before), that the certificate was issued and will be sent to us today.

"For me that was a moment of a slight cross-cultural shock. Why? In most countries in the world public administration in such cases is not responding to applicants by email. In most countries I know, they will never address the applicant with first name only. And finally most of the administrative units I know, will never react to a reminder phone call, by responding to the request within two working days, knowing there is a queue of other cases waiting...

"So, that was a positive example. To balance, a negative example follows. Stories about uneducated doctors are a separate topic at all meetings of immigrants in Norway.

"My wife was bitten by a tick, she had all the initial symptoms of Lyme disease, including a large (around 10 cm diameter) purple circle around the bite. We went to the hospital emergency department (this was on a Sunday). The young doctor first did the most amazing thing. He took a blue pen and drew a large circle around this purple contusion ... We didn't know, until today, what this blue circle was intended to demonstrate. Later on, he opened Google and started looking for pictures of similar bites... well... no comment.

"After some minutes, he said that he cannot prescribe any antibiotics in these circumstances, because my wife for sure had no Lyme disease. Paracet should help, he said (paracetamol is the standard treatment for 90% of all illnesses in Norway...). We asked an obvious question - how could he be so sure? The answer was simple 'Norwegian ticks have no borreliosis (Lyme disease)!'

"Finally, after an extensive discussion, we forced him to prescribe an antibiotic. He was looking for an advanced medicine in his very secret book and finally said, that he will prescribe a very modern antibiotic. We looked at the printed prescription: Ampicillin... (in use since 1961)"

*

As in Bart's example it often surprises me to meet the friendliness of people in public administration in Norway. I have discussed it with my husband a few times and asked myself the question, why is that? My only conclusion would be that people are happy at work...

What Bart's stories also illustrate, is that he notices what people in his new country have become blind to. People take for granted that the police will be polite to you, and they are used to getting paracetamol for almost any illness...

What have you become blind to in your own culture? (You could ask a foreigner for his or her views)

There is a lot of negative media attention on the challenges of immigration, particularly in the cases of South Asians and Africans immigrating to Europe; integration problems, unemployment, ghettos, crime.

The total picture is not all that negative, of course, as there are also many benefits, of which Lasse Ostervold has some examples to share. Lasse is Norwegian, has a Bachelor of Arts in Anthropology and Environmental Change, and is a self-employed Mental Health Care Worker and Adventurer. Among many various tasks, Lasse has worked as a polar bear guard, meaning his job was to look out for polar bears during expeditions in Svalbard - a Norwegian archipelago in the Arctic Ocean. You will find Lasse's link to a filmed 2-min adventure with a curious polar bear in the reference list.

"I believe that one can learn a lot from other cultures, and the people who immigrate to Norway. We tend to ignore knowledge from both cultures and our own history in our attempt to modernize our culture. Two examples come to mind.

"With the modernization of the country, and its wealth, the structure of the extended family has disappeared. I have noticed that people in the Pakistani communities do not bring their elderly to senior homes; their grandmothers and grandfathers remain with the family. As a fact, the percentage of Pakistani families using the elderly services in the west of Oslo where I live, is .. 0%. Families prefer to take the burden to take care of their own elders. It is in strong contrast to the Norwegian model, which sadly seems to lead to too many elderly people feeling lonely and dying alone, while their family tend to spend more and more time increasing their wealth. Maybe there could be another model? What if we learn from other countries that care for their family members? What if we combine this model of love and care with our own model of economics where women are more involved in the workforce than in any other place in the world? Can we find a combined solution? I believe we can.

Innovations have proven that we no longer need huge bureaucracies to control the masses. The company eBay has shown us that control can be managed between buyer and seller. Quality is easily controlled by the user of the system through the user's own reflection of how trustworthy the seller is. And, it works! What if we gave the elderly or the disabled the same opportunity to choose themselves where and how to live, and we leave it up to each provider of service to hire staff ? Why not let companies hire family members or other people for the receiver of service trust or love? It might feel better to have someone around that you know, rather than unfamiliar caretakers with a turnover of 2-3 times per day. The economic cost for society would be the same, but the gross value of love would rise. To die with dignity is indeed a human right, and a system to force loneliness is so the very opposite of that. The last breath we take in this life is the very moment of truth. To die alone and unloved is indeed the most tragic way to leave this world. Failure of even one individual in our society being able to do so, is a total failure as a whole. I think Norway has created a society of individualism, and the cost we all pay is in the currency of loneliness. When suicidal people are asked why they no longer want to live, loneliness is the number one key factor. So, lets change it.

"Once I was hired to accompany a person to Portugal. He had suffered brain damage after a traffic accident. He suffered daily from extreme uncontroled anger. During the week that we were in Portugal, we spent time in a small village on the south coast. In this wonderful little village he was never treated as an outcast. Every person met him with love, passion, laughter, a bit of food, a little to drink. He did not understand a word but, he understood the fact that he was treated with love. That week he was all smiles, only a few 'accidents' where I had to remove him from minor situations. When we returned back to Norway, he changed the minute we arrived; he became very nervous and he wasn't smiling anymore. Already at the airport he went totally mad. He was back to being treated as an outsider, someone with a scary look. It makes me wonder, have we lost the ability to treat people with compassion? Has our trust in professionals and medicine removed our selves from our very soul? Have we become so institutionalized that we don't pay attention to people's feelings and wellbeing, that we consider our outsiders like unpeople? We move them to an institution, so they are hidden from society. They are met by professionals, taken away from love and care.

"This is where I notice a difference with other cultures, and that the immigrants can enrich Norwegian society, particularly on how we treat our loved ones, our elderly and people with disabilities - whether it is mental or physical. I would quite like to import the ideas of Bhutan. In Bhutan they measure national wealth in Gross National Happiness (GNH) rather than in Gross Domestic Product (GDP)! In a globalized world, lets all learn from each other, and help to build societies built on love and care."

The figure below is drawn from Eurostat 2013 data that shows immigration in a selection of countries in Europe.

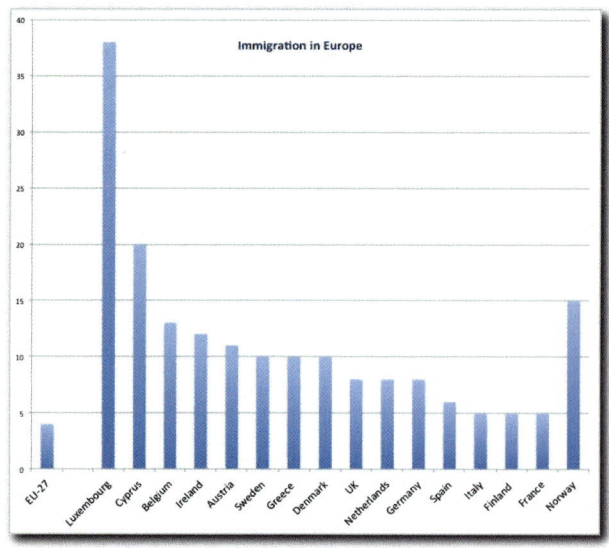

*

From immigration to international business… We are living in busy times, everything has accelerated, and we have never been closer and more contactable. Also in this area, cultural differences impact on us and can create challenging situations when we work with other cultures. The article that follows, published in *Diversity Journal* 6 July 2012, was inspired by the stress I felt from my last corporate job, a business client, and fellow entrepreneurs.

Work-Life Balance in a Global Context

Work/life balance, WLB, work - and life balance. "A beloved child has many names," is a Norwegian saying. But some companies avoid talking about this subject, for fear of opening Pandora's box and hearing how people are really doing, thinking they cannot meet the employees' expectations and wishes.

A progressive company would want its staff to be healthy and therefore would consider work/life balance as an important factor of its vision for people and performance. However, in an international company it can be quite tricky to set rules of good work-life balance, as the cultural practices vary enormously. Is it okay to arrange meetings in the evenings or start an international meeting a Monday morning? Can you require workers to respond over the weekend? Can you request that someone postpones their holiday due to an urgent issue? It really depends on the culture. In Norway you would probably get a clear and loud no to postponing someone's holiday and in Dubai it wouldn't be an issue to work over the weekend as theirs isn't Saturday/Sunday.

And when it comes to holidays, well, you can't implement a *company holiday* due to legal reasons. In France workers in large enterprises enjoy eight weeks' leave (five weeks + compensation for working 40 hours in a 35 work-week system). In the Netherlands employees in certain sectors work a 36-hour week, and can get compensation in holidays if they work 40 hours. This is opposed to the United States which has no law granting employees holidays-although two weeks is fairly common, and Hong Kong where you get one-two week's paid leave depending on your length of service.

Then there is the individual aspect. Some people live to work, and some people work to live. Baby Boomers and Generation Y may have different views on what work/life balance means. Some people have very clear opinions on what they want and don't want, and others are influenced by their surroundings. One is not better than the other; all have strengths and something to contribute to the company. As people are social animals, I believe we are rather influenced by our cultural, company, and family standards. An example: a person lives in a national culture where friend and family time is valued and work should not interfere with this time. She grows up in a family of 'over-achievers' and starts working in a company where long hours are expected. Two factors against one - family and company against national culture. And where is the individual preference? It can be hard to differentiate with three influences at the same time. Because we are often influenced by our surroundings, I believe a company has an ethical obligation to promote work/life balance. In the end it serves the company with retention, productivity and morale.

So what could an international company do?

- o Follow the various laws of the host country, and accept them e.g. a team with people who have eight weeks and two weeks of holiday respectively may feel some jealousy and irritation; this has to be dealt with.
- o There needs to be an understanding from the top management of the relationship between work/life balance and financial performance.
- o Train managers in stress management
- o Agree on a meeting culture that would suit most people; no business travel during weekends.
- o Conduct a survey, in order to understand what most people want to be motivated by and manage their entire lives (e.g. working from home, evening meetings, travel).

- o In teams keep open dialogues about workload and share and cooperate whenever possible.
- o Have honest conversations about what work/life balance means to the individual.

Global context or national context, in the end, a company wants high-performing staff and employees want an enjoyable and healthy workplace.

*

Still on the work arena, I had an interesting discussion with a fellow entrepreneur about presentation skills and how they differ from country to country. It inspired me to write the following blog.

Presentation Skills Seen Through a Cultural View

I attended a training session where the facilitator gave us the following task; *Think of a great speaker and name her/him*. The Americans among us couldn't think of any, and the facilitator said; "That's because you Americans are such good speakers, all of you!".

It is true, Americans *are* really good at presenting. So why is that? Probably because they are educated to present from early on in their lives.

In a setting where you have the luxury to see many different nationalities present at the same time, it is quite interesting to see how language and culture shine through. Sharing some recent personal experiences; for example a Frenchman spoke in long and complicated sentences that sometimes led us off the subject (known to like complexity), the German kept physical distance to the audience (respecting personal space), the American went straight to the point (time is money) and the Australian sat down with us (informal and laid-back).

It also made me think of an international seminar I went to where, of I-don't-know-how-many presentations I saw, there were probably 2-3 people who did a great job on slides, voice, content, movement and eye contact. It puzzled me that people at this level (mostly leaders and speakers) have not received some kind of presentation training. It's like people should just know how to do it. But, actually, outside the US, not many learn these skills at school - UK probably being part of the exception with their debating clubs. Considering that public speaking rates very high on any scale of stress and anxiety, and it is an important part of business life, it is probably a good idea to include presentation skills as part of basic education. One could take the approach that this kind of training should be the business world's job, and many companies do offer it. However, speaking in public comes in at so many aspects of life that I would vote for the first option.

I would suggest the following as a presentation guideline that would work with several nationalities:

- Look at your audience
- Speak at a speed that people can follow, particularly if you have an international group
- Don't overcrowd your slides, let people be able to read what is there
- Depending on the audience, have someone check the text beforehand
- If you choose to have no slides, write some key points on a flipchart so that the visual memory listeners get some tags to remember your speech by
- Ask for feedback by trusted people so that you can constantly improve and learn.

This next blog is as much about women as it is about culture. The examples are from France, but I am sure many women will have similar examples from other countries.

Cultural Differences, Women and Men

The other day I met with a group of women working in a large international enterprise. Together with a co-member, I had just made a presentation about PWN Global, an international network for professional women, and we had the opportunity to talk with people afterwards around some snacks and drinks.

Since there were several nationalities, we started talking about challenges for women with a cultural twist.

A couple of us as foreign women in France had observed that there is a tendency for men to comment about women - behind their backs as well as straight to their faces. My own personal example of that is the comments I get from men I barely know, about my femininity and style, my clothing, my weight, and my hair. The women around the circle commented; "You have to give them back the same!" "Fight back!" I agree, one has to do that. However, it sounds similar to the dilemma of *blaming the victim*... as if it's the woman's fault if she feels uncomfortable because she doesn't speak up!?

Have to be rude, because others are rude. Hit because other people hit. Yes, one has to sometimes, but is the world getting any better from that? And what about personal values? I, for one, don't like to be rude, so why should I be forced to behave that way?

A male business associate of mine observed a cultural difference on this topic when moving back to France after ten years abroad. He started noticing all the comments the women got in the office, and how uncomfortable they looked. He concluded that it must drain them of energy over time. Several mature (by that I mean age 30 and above) women I have talked with say the contrary, that they are used to it.

A young Norwegian student in Paris has written a blog about the same topic - being overwhelmed by all the comments she gets. It is the second blog I have read in a short time period that talks about the problem of being groped in the Métro in Paris. Additionally, this student mentions the fact that men don't *allow* her to eat what she wants to eat, because she should "keep her slim line". She finds it all very tiring and intimidating, and due to that can no longer imagine staying in France when she has completed her studies.

Notice the difference of age. The mature women say; "You have to make the same remarks to them", "You get used to it", "You have to learn to fight back and be rude". The young one says, "I won't take it, I will leave". Food for thought…

I am mature, but I still find the comments annoying and I have difficulty in being rude back - it's against my values. I think women need help from men who understand. And maybe we women in France - probably other countries too - can learn to take a different approach; "Why do you say such things, how would you feel if you got comments like that all day?" Maybe some people would get it..? Bon, where there is life, there is hope!

*

From women in France to how different nationalities approach domestic animals. Here's a little story about my pretty dog's international encounters. For me it illustrates that we might do things differently, but we share many of the same interests and intent.

National Culture and The People Magnet

We have a People-Magnet in the house. The magnet is called Ben, a Golden Retriever, he attracts people from all corners of the world. It is quite interesting to see how culture influences the way everyone approaches him - and the person at the other end of the lead.

Living in Southern France, at times we meet quite a lot of tourists. Here is a summary of the generalities that I have experienced from the nationalities we typically meet around where we live.

The Italians: Start pointing at a distance, come over, ask if they can take a picture, sit down and give him a good rub all over. Say loudly that he is very pretty.

The French: The young generation: Talk about him at a distance, come over and ask if they can touch him and then tell him how beautiful he is. Children tend to just touch him in passing. The others: Walk straight over to him, give him a kiss - or several - and tell me how adorable he is.

The British: Ask politely if they can touch him, sit down to pet him, talk a bit with him and then thank me.

The Germans and the Dutch: They smile, nod to me and may say that I have a beautiful dog.

The Americans (don't know which states they are from): Talk loudly about him at a distance, then come over and pet him while they tell me about their dog back home.

The Asians (I should ask people what country they are from): Politely ask if they can take a picture of the dog, and then with the dog. They pat him gently on the head.

The approach is different, the interest, the love and the smiles are the same.

*

Closing out this chapter on national culture, I would like to share extracts of a story from Ozozoma Sokoh, who has previously written for her employer's expatriate department about her experiences on living in The Netherlands. Ozozoma is a Nigerian geologist and a cookbook writer. Her blog is well known in food-lover circles and she has given a talk about Nigerian food on TEDx Port Harcourt. Links are to be found in the list of references.

"Nothing quite prepares you for the adventures you'll have when you make the decision to move both home and country. After a few years of living in the Netherlands, I've come to realise that being enamoured of tulips is not sufficient reason to make life-changing moves! Before we moved, I'd visited the Netherlands many times and each time one aspect or another of Dutch life wowed me. I will be honest though; the fact that it was a flat country and perfect for cycling was not one of them. Stroopwafels (syrup waffles) might have been one because for me, there's no better reason to travel than food - it broadens the mind as well as the waistline.

"The first thing to hit us when we arrived at the airport on a typical spring morning in April was the cold. Some time down the road my husband and I (heavily pregnant), and our two girls were happy, and had quickly settled into 'walking' (i.e. the girls were hand-carried) everywhere. What a difference! For the first time in years we didn't have a car and my husband's back suffered for it - see the girls, were not used to walking; at home in Nigeria they were chauffeured from pillar to post, so this was new. After weeks of trials, we bought a double buggy and life eased up, except when getting on and off the trams! (Three years on, the girls will walk miles for ice cream or less.)

"If you've never heard of Dutch directness, you must come to the Netherlands and experience it for yourself. One hears of the almost-rude Dutchman, who will speak his mind with neither thought nor care for those on the receiving end. However, for us it has been a joy to live in a society where you know where you stand with people, with no open ended comments and certainly few instances that could be misconstrued or misinterpreted. This is my take-away, nicely boxed up in the new 'me' - this ability to speak my mind and be honest with myself, learning perhaps even to say no - perhaps not with the force of those born with the gift, but still… learning!

"It has been great fun learning to speak the language. I have found myself in love with the guttural Gs and the conjugations of Dutch verbs - don't ask me why. On a good note, learning Dutch has done numerous things for me - I only wish I had done it sooner. When we first arrived, before our son was born, our camera went bonkers and we took it to the shop for repairs. A few days later, we received a note that I interpreted as the document of 'receipt'. After a few weeks we eventually headed to the shop to pick the camera up. It turns out that the document of 'receipt' was in fact a statement of readiness for collection! I do hope the son never asks for his baby pics..."

Final remarks

"The world is getting smaller," we say. We travel more. We buy products from every corner of the world - at home. We travel abroad to work. We work in companies that either have headquarters in another country or in organisations that are connected to other countries for internal or external reasons. Cultural influence is everywhere!

Yet, it is interesting to note that many companies do not offer cultural training to their staff. Many a project and business deal has failed because of this. When I started in an international organization in 2001, there was no cultural training offered to the large amount of staff in international roles. I, as many others, learnt by doing (sometimes failing but always learning).

Working with many different nationalities at the same time, is not the same as having lived abroad once or twice. An example could be reading emails from a variety of nationalities. Many will translate their mother tongue into English, and the style might come across differently than intended. The reader needs to know this, and check understanding when in doubt, instead of taking the message negatively - which is often the case, unfortunately.

And... national culture is complex; how can you separate what is personality or other cultural influences like gender, education, generation, geography, etc.? I remember being challenged in a workshop on cultural differences where a French lady said; "All of that could be my personality, not my culture". I explained that understanding the main rules and regulations of a country is helpful, an example being that you have to take off your shoes when you enter a private home in Norway. Maybe in ten out of a thousand homes it would be okay to walk inside with your shoes, but in 990 cases you are most likely to upset the host. As a business person, this is also interesting, as there is a market for selling slippers! The French lady was right, however, we still need to check individual differences when working with people from different countries. We are complex beings, with unique experiences that influence how we see the world and how we behave.

Richard D Lewis, British interculturalist, linguist, and author of eight books on cross-cultural communication, has made the following observation about national culture:

- "Gaining the allegiance of people at international level with people who do not share the same values, customs, habits, aspirations, preferences, rules and laws is difficult.
- "The manager who is unaware of or chooses to ignore the manner in which certain cultures are motivated does so at a *big risk*".

What is your national culture? How does it show up at work and in your relationships with people of other cultures? (If you reply; "I just treat people with respect and act normal", it is likely that you would benefit from asking for feedback from someone with another cultural background.)

CHAPTER FIVE:
GENDER AND FREEDOM

"We've begun to raise daughters more like sons... but few have the courage to raise our sons more like our daughters." - Gloria Steinem

There is enough information and discussion around that shows that having more women in senior positions produces better performing companies, so why is it taking so long to get more women up in the ranks? It is a complex question with many possible answers. One being, change takes time. Women and men like to stay within their comfort zone and keep things as they know them - it feels safer that way.

A lot of positive change *has* happened in the last fifty years, when it comes to talking about equality, respect for people and justice. But there is still much to do. Regarding gender equality, I react when I hear someone say that any woman anywhere could become CEO if she wants, that it's women's *choice* to dress half-naked in music videos and that women covered in niqab say they *choose* to follow their religion. I know these three examples will trigger various reactions, they all have some tension related to them, and they are all complex. I would like to invite you to reflect on; what is *want to* versus real *possibility*, what is *choice* and what is *freedom*? How much do we do by own will versus doing what we are expected to do? I would argue that it is difficult to judge what is real personal choice, as we are surrounded by stereotyped attitudes in society, norms and guidelines (with cultural variations), and it colours us in so many ways.

I remember from my early teens that I started questioning female and male behaviour; what is learnt behaviour and what is biology? I noticed that I was somewhat different than many other girls and realised that my role models were my three elder brothers and a mother who was the head of the family and did not shy away from physical work. I came to the conclusion that there is a lot that is learnt behaviour, guided by what a girl and a boy are expected to do, according to a society's gender mental model. Whether we want it or not, we are more or less influenced by both visible and invisible societal pressures and expectations.

In many countries there are still traditional expectations of women: generally speaking, being a good mother, looking good, soft spoken, stay home or possibly work as a nurse or nanny, and take care of all the housework. A woman acting out of the box meets skepticism and/or criticism, both in the private sphere and at work. Men also have expectations, and also face stereotypes, for example in choosing a *manly* profession, being the family provider or have a higher salary than the wife, be strong, take charge, know how to *fix things*, and preferably not show too much emotion. They might meet skepticism if they choose a profession that is considered *female*. There are however less blocks and behaviour expectations if they choose to climb the career ladder.

Clearly many businesses and many countries have a more liberal outlook on gender expectations and gender equality. It isn't all as black and white as I have described above, but I keep facing old attitudes and lots and lots of blind spots, and it surprises me. I thought we had moved on. I can understand, however, that when you are in a majority situation (e.g. male leader among other male leaders) it's hard to see the challenges of those in the minority. Being told the reality of the minority may feel like criticism and being blamed.

I have mentioned stereotypes a few times. For clarity: what is a stereotype and what is a generalisation? According to the Oxford English dictionary a stereotype is; *A widely held but fixed and oversimplified image or idea of a particular type of person or thing: e.g. the stereotype of the woman as the carer.*

Valid generalisations, however, are supported by facts and proven with several examples. For a cultural group, for example, one generalises what is true for approximately 80% of the population.

Linked to stereotypes and generalisations, the term *unconscious bias* has become prominent in the language of diversity. It basically means that we are not aware that we stereotype others, that we are unconscious of it. There is a well-known test created by Harvard University where you can test your own implicit opion/unconscious bias (the link is in the reference list), which can lead to surprising and maybe not so welcome results. We tend to be more biased than we would like to admit. If you consider the preface of this book, the parable of the blind men and the elephant, one could make the link that we are blind to our own biases, and this prevents us from seeking a more complete understanding of the nature of things.

"I stick to my opinion. Please do not confuse me with facts!"
- Unknown

We meet stereotypes, unconscious bias and generalisations both privately and at work. Daily I read about *women want this, men want that* on social media, and in certain types of newspapers. Would you call that a generalisation or a stereotype? There seems to be a large share of superficial descriptions of men and women's likes and wishes, so I would therefore call it stereotyping. The research company Catalyst's research on gender, leadership and stereotypes (*Different Cultures; Similar Perceptions, 2006*), suggests that we expect certain behaviours, certain educational and career choices, certain looks. This can be a straitjacket for both men and women, and I do think it limits us and reduces creativity.

We have talked about *adapting the women* for a while, while these days we see a wave of *engaging the men*. Catalyst mentions in a report about engaging men in gender equality, that there are three factors that hinder men from becoming gender champions: apathy, fear, and ignorance. (*Catalyst report: Engaging Men in Gender Initiatives, Part 1, 2009*) Unfortunately, there are some people who do firmly defend their walls and their world (out of fear?), without trying to lean outside the walls and see what it looks like. My intent, as a D&I practitioner, and many people like me, is to achieve a better world for men and women, not turning the coin to give all advantages to and favour women. The fact is, though, that we still live in a world where in many cases men are (possibly unconsciously) favoured over women in such things as promotions, challenging and developing projects, and pay. It would be good if we could all embrace this as indeed a fact, and not as a criticism or a threat that men will be disfavoured. Helping to create a fair world for both men and women, means that both genders need to be involved.

Senior women have been criticized for not advancing or supporting other women in the career pipeline. Some say the thinking behind that is: "I made it here without help, so I won't make it easier for you !" It has also been argued that women at that level are too competitive and do not want other females to join them. It might be true, and I personally think the dynamics change when it is more common for a company to have several women at the top. There is power in numbers. And it is no joke that three is a magical number. Get three women in your leadership team, and women are no longer categorized as the *token women*. They are then seen as individuals with individual opinions and strengths.

Another criticism of female managers is that some use their sexuality, or their charm, to climb the career ladder. Dana-Leigh Strauss, Corporate Manager in the UK, has shared a story on this with me:

"We often speak of male chauvinism. That in the professional, corporate world men have a club that excludes women. This generalisation is true and can be attested to by experience. But isn't the sole reason why women, at times, aren't respected at work.

"Having been posted there from the United Kingdom, I remember when I worked in Australia for a global corporation that I was surprised that I was one of the most senior women in the organisation. I was not particularly senior by European standards, in fact - just middle management. But by Australian standards because there were so few women in senior positions, I was one of the most senior. I was a member of a project team and remember clearly that women were not invited into meetings by the senior male managers. Males, at an equivalent level to mine, were invited to the meetings but not any of the women.

"However, over time, I noticed that there was one woman who started to attend the senior manager meetings. Her business sense was not remarkable, but she was hardworking and very ambitious. She was quite adept at getting her own way and if she disagreed with another person's point of view, she did her utmost to undermine the other person and their idea. I remember silently coining the term 'idea assassin' to describe her behaviour. She was attractive and dressed quite sedately - trousers, a blouse, a tidy sweater and perhaps a scarf. Except for when she wanted something - and then her style of dress changed. Out came the plunging necklines and the short skirts. There seemed to be a direct correlation or link amongst her changing style of dress, her ambition, and her attendance at meetings with senior managers. Hence, the observation about male chauvinism that excludes women and a female who behaved in such way that reduces respect for women in the workplace. It's not only the men who are to blame."

Women in politics and the corporate world do receive disproportionate attention on what clothes they wear, sometimes to a ridiculous level. However, as Dana-Leigh's story illustrates, if women want to be heard and valued for their skills and competencies, dressing for the job is also of importance. In my opinion, seeing too many private parts (and that goes for both men *and* women) disturbs the professional setting and intentions may be misinterpreted.

*

I discussed expectations of men and women with Devika Eifert (Polish-Canadian), a psychologist and writer in Canada. Below she shares a story on what is expected of a son versus a daughter:

"Sons Are Special, Daughters Serve. My childhood friend Stella and I come from families of several sisters and one brother. Reconnecting after three decades, we naturally asked about each other's family. When we spoke of our brothers, up came the topic of how The Son had always been special to our mothers, not because of who they were or anything they did, but simply by virtue of being a son.

" 'She's 93' Stella said, 'So I drive across town three times a week to the nursing home, go to special shops to buy the Polish treats she likes, talk to her, keep in touch with the staff, etc. etc. Does she appreciate it? No. She expects it. That's what a daughter is supposed to do. My brother lives closer by, shows up once a month, if that, with a paper cup of coffee, stays for fifteen minutes, yet all she can talk about is Eddie this and Eddie that! It's totally unfair, but what irks me most is that it still bothers me. Yet truth is I don't want to leave her there alone.'

"Weeks later Stella called me and said that her mom surprisingly had asked for me. I had never been close to her, but figured if that old a person asks for you, you ought to go right away and was glad I did, for she died within a few weeks.

"We found her sitting in that heartbreakingly silent circle of neglected elderly people that typically congregate around the nurses' station. She got so excited when we greeted her that even blind as she was, she literally picked up her walker and stomped in front of us, repeating 'Boy oh boy! Boy oh boy!' all the way down the long hall. It was quite a sight.

"Once in her room she matter-of-factly accepted all the special foods Stella brought her. Then later on while speaking of the past she had shared with my mother in post WW2 refugee camps, she began to cry. Her faithful daughter handed her the nearby box of Kleenex. The moment it was in her mother's hands, she suddenly stopped crying, held it up like some sacred object and with shocking adoration said, "Eddie gave me this."

"' See! This is exactly what I was talking about!' It was not her mouth but Stella's dramatic eye roll in front of her blind mother that said it, while my raised eyebrows said, 'A Kleenex box? That one takes the cake!' This time the son's special behavior was so blatantly ludicrous that we both had to hold our hands over our mouth to keep from bursting out laughing.

"P.S. I sent this story to a dear friend, a fellow writer, who emailed a very wise response. 'Of course!' I exclaimed to the computer screen, palm slapping against my forehead. 'How could I not have thought of this?! It's an absolutely necessary part of the story - especially in a book on Diversity & Inclusion.'

"Here is what he wrote: 'I loved your page on Sons ... Of course there is another side to the page. I spent a good part of my life trying to survive that Special Relationship that Moms have with their sons. Until a particular wake-up incident when I was forty, I never understood why it had always felt as if I was in a fight for my life when it came to Mom.'

"Now I sit here reflecting ... how easy it is to slip into non-inclusiveness, however unintentionally, simply by neglecting 'another side of the page'."

*

Devika's story reminds me of the Catalyst report I mentioned earlier (*Different Cultures; Similar Perceptions, 2006*). They found out that the perceived two top leadership strengths for men were *Problem Solving* and

Influencing Upwards, while for women *Supporting* and *Consulting*. The stereotypes that come out of this are; *Women Take Care, Men Take Charge*.

Many will expect a woman to fill the role of caretaker in all relationships: children, husband, parents, brothers/sisters, even at work - it's in women's genes, right? Maybe, maybe not. I'm wondering, aren't we women keeping that ball rolling by accepting and fulfilling this role? My opinion is that it is a gift to know you can help others, as long as life is in balance - and this goes for both men and women. As Devika points out after the response of her friend to her story, both sides of the coin of stereotyped expectations - whether it is *take care or take charge* can feel like a burden, in different ways.

You have probably noticed that when you or maybe your company go through a change process, at times it feels like taking one step forward and two steps back. That's also what I see in my line of work. There is progress and then it seems like it's all going the wrong way…

I got that feeling when I read the comments to an article that asked some well-founded questions regarding the lack of female top managers in the private sector in the European Nordics. It inspired me to write a blog about it.

What If…

I read an article in November 2014 in *The Economist*, the headline being 'A Nordic Mystery'. The text was interesting, asking why there weren't more women in top positions in the private sector in these countries that are considered the most egalitarian in the world. This blog will focus on the 98 comments that followed…

Some of them suggested that women don't want to be managers, and some said that women prefer to stay at home. I don't disagree, some women don't want to be managers, and some women do prefer to stay at home - but what about men? Wouldn't you think that some of them are also happy where they are, without wanting to fight to get to the top? Wouldn't you think some of them also would like to have shorter days at work and go home to play with their children? I'm amazed at the fact that a fair number of people seem to think that all men or all women are wired the same way.
I feel like taking this world in my hand, shake it around a few times and see where the pieces will fall, without the history of the old world.

That old world was made up of men being in the majority at work (with the consequence that the rules of the game were made by and for men). The old world didn't allow women to have an education. The old world thought women didn't have a brain that functioned as well as men's. The old world also thought Africans were lesser humans.

Things have changed in the meantime, in most parts of the world.

What if the new world could be even *more* different? What if men and women could just be who they are? What if there was a world where typical male and typical female traits were seen to be *as good and as important*? Where a masculine woman and a feminine man were just as normal as *any other combination of traits*? A world where many different kind of roads would lead to success? (Without the lists of *This is how you have to be to make it in life*) What if a company would stop expecting their top managers to work eighty hours a week? What if we looked at profit in a different way?

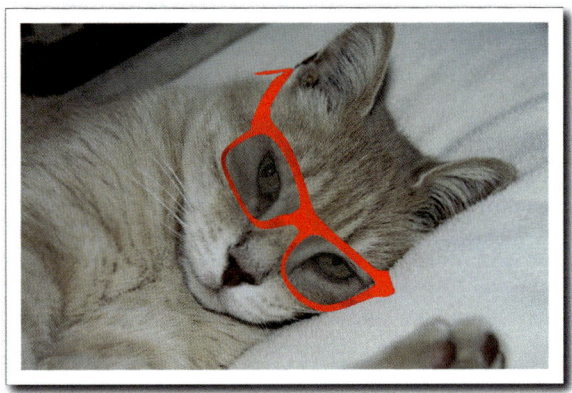

When I read the comments under *The Economist* article, I must admit I felt rather frustrated; so many stereotypes, so many simplifications of *what women really want*, so many *old truths*. (Since then I have read several similar articles with similar comments, unfortunately.) I was pleased, however, that not all the comments were what I would categorize as old school. One of the commenters suggested that if we think a CEO or senior executive equals someone who has ruthless ambition and bullies others, then yes, you will get mostly men going for that kind of a job, men of a certain type.

Looking at the big picture, women and men in this time of history - in large parts of the world - have more possibilities to choose a career of their liking and to be authentic at work. However, we still have a long way to go for full acceptance of various skill sets and strengths, plus there is still too much stereotyped thinking.

*

Regarding stereotypes and expected behaviours (and skills), I would like to share this amusing story told by Lesley Brook, Director of BrookGraham in the UK:

"Our rather high-tech kitchen tap has developed a leak, so I called the tap manufacturer's after sales support team to get advice.

A woman answered the phone, told me what to do to find out where exactly the leak was, and said that once I knew that she'd be able to tell me which little valve/connector I needed to buy. She said she'd send me the diagram about how to fit it, and 'it's dead easy to do yourself in five minutes. You don't need a plumber.'

Having done the checks and isolated the source of the leak, I phoned back to order the part. This time I ot a male call centre operator. He ordered the part, and said: 'I'll send you the diagram to give to your plumber.' !! "

Different expectations of skills...

Touching both the subject of culture and of gender, the ban on Burqa and implemented in France triggered a variety of viewpoints and discussions.

Burqa and Niqab Ban in France

On 11th April 2011 France implemented a ban on wearing burqa and niqab in public places. The same day two women were arrested while they were demonstrating against the new law - apparently due to an illegal demonstration, not because they were veiled. Several Muslim French citizens have voiced that they feel discriminated against and one could say that the situation was tense. I would like to shed some light on different perspectives in the variety of discussions that went on.

First of all, why do Muslim women wear a burqa or niqab? According to the Qur'an, men and women should dress modestly - which means a woman is not obliged to be completely veiled (several scholars of Islam have confirmed this). However, as Mohammed's wives covered their faces, one could say that you show even more faith and modesty by covering up completely. Across the Muslim nations and branches, from Morocco to Indonesia, the view on what is modest differs a lot, and I would think local customs also play a role.

According to writer John J. O'Neill, the burka and niqab started becoming a practise due to Caliphs and Sultans stealing other men's women. Hiding their women's beauty was a necessity to keep them from being kidnapped, not a religiously inspired rule. Not everyone agrees with Mr O'Neill, referring for example to verses 33:59 in the Qu'ran: *"O Prophet, tell your wives and your daughters and the women of the believers to bring down over themselves [part] of their outer garments. That is more suitable that they will be known and not be abused. And ever is Allah Forgiving and Merciful."* This quote is taken from the website Quran.com Surat Al-'Ahzab (The Combined Forces). Apparently there are several translations with slightly different wording, and the verses may be, and are, interpreted differently.

Adding a personal note to this particular translation; *That they will be known* is kind of hard in a niqab or burka. Either way, my understanding is that there is some religious guidance for women regarding covering oneself to a certain degree. To which degree is the root of the discussion and it leads to cultural complications in a globalized world.

So why did this ban come into place in France? Plainly speaking - because a veiled woman cannot be identified. This creates some tricky situations - how can a kindergarten teacher know that she or he hands over the right child to the right mother or how can a social worker or a banker be sure that she or he gives out money to the right person? Additionally, it speaks against French values, the value of equality (men do not veil themselves, so why should women?).

What about freedom to dress how you want? The Muslim women who were demonstrating against the law said that it is their choice to be veiled, and why should the government decide what people should wear? Protesters voice that they feel Muslim women are singled out and stigmatized - and a reaction could be that even more women would want to veil themselves to protest against this stigmatization.

Then we have the feminist angle. "Why should women cover themselves completely and not men?" "What choice are you talking about, these women are brainwashed". Veiling women is seen as an extension of male control over women's lives, and other women should stand up to speak for them. In France there is an association called *Ni Putes Ni Soumises (Neither Whores Nor Submissives)* which is led by French muslim women of North African descent. Their goal is to put light on the violence against immigrant women in France. This group supports the ban of burqa and niqab.

To look at it with a practical eye, an advantage is that a woman is not looked upon by men (not everyone likes to be called after on the street, which actually happens in many places). A disadvantage is that your skin is not exposed to the sun and you get a lack of Vitamin D (unless you have a private court yard where you can unveil).

The above are some of the views and angles I have seen over a period of time. I think they represent real examples of the complexity of diversity and inclusion. Since 2011 not much has happened, the police doesn't have the resources to follow up on the law, but they can if they choose to where they see a conflict situation.

*

I mentioned early on that it was a bit of a culture shock to move from Scandinavia to Mediterranean France (via the US). I have found that it is just a matter of time and experience to learn what works regarding the cultural and practical differences, but where I struggle is on gender differences. This links back to my values of equality and justice.

The following blog was written by the request of my husband, as he thought the story illustrates well that one goes blind to what is a habit, "just the way it always has been", in a culture. This story is not unique for France. After I wrote the blog I got several comments from women having experienced similar hotel situations in other countries, such as Switzerland and UK.

Sometimes We Just Need Someone to Shed Light on a Situation

The other day my husband said: "You should write about that hotel story, I didn't even think about it until you pointed it out."

So here goes the hotel story. We had received a gift card that we could use in different hotels around France. We chose a hotel-castle in a beautiful region called Midi-Pyrénées. Driving around the city of Rodez you see castles every five minutes (almost!) and picturesque villages, many of them voted 'most beautiful villages in France.

I took care of the booking; one night via the gift card arrangement and one night via booking.com. I also had some correspondence directly with the hotel. The castle was beautiful and we had a very nice stay. When leaving, the hotel director asked how we liked it and asked us if we could please rate them on booking.com. I noticed that he only spoke to my husband, and he seemed annoyed when I spoke, but I pushed it aside as my being too sensitive.

However… a few days later I rated them on booking.com and I additionally received a rating request directly from the hotel, addressed to "Monsieur Heggertveit-Aoudia" (who doesn't exist since this is my maiden name connected to my married name). That's when I got upset and also rather puzzled; how can they ignore half of their guests? This is a place where mostly couples go, but they only ask the man for feedback. After I had calmed down a bit, I wrote back kindly suggesting that they send their feedback requests to "Monsieur ou Madame" or "Monsieur et Madame". In this way they include all their guests, yet can use their standardized version. I also informed them that foreign guests would find their approach rather impolite. To date they have not responded to my feedback.

I find it amazing. I did the booking, I did the correspondence, we both stayed at the hotel, yet they are only interested in my husband's opinion. They rule out half of their clients! (BIG sales mistake, I'd say)

I have mentioned this story to a few people, and indeed, the French people I have talked with say that it is not unusual here and they don't really think about it. When I point it out, however, they do see that it is rather strange.

It is a detail or 'a pebble'. But, 'pebbles' can become a mountain.

*

Still in France, it was an interesting time being in the country throughout the *DSK case* (May/June 2011), which made me write the following:

Affaire DSK: Positive Effects

It is difficult NOT to speak about Dominique Strauss-Kahn (former Managing Director of IMF - International Monetary Fond) these days. I will not talk about his innocence or otherwise, that is up to the court. I will however talk about some interesting 'side effects' of this whole affair.

First of all, the interest about what happened between a possible president-to-be and a chambermaid is massive. The sales of magazines and newspapers in France went up like a rocket in the weeks after DSK was arrested. There were TV specials, live feed from the court in the US (even via SMS to the TV journalist!) and numerous debate programmes. One point of interest is that this is a man in a powerful position, a world leader, a possible president. The other is that it is rather symbolic; *the white, rich man being opposed by a poor, black woman.*

Not long after DSK's arrest, another French politician had to step down due to allegations of sexual harassment - said to be a result of the DSK affair as the women got the courage to speak up.

As the story continues, the debates develop. Many questions are raised about unfriendly working environments for women in politics. Interviews are made of leading women who inform that they cannot wear skirts at work due to the comments they get. There are women who have sent written complaints about harassment at work that are never shed light on. Warning signs are coming up about 'old school attitudes' that men 'seduce', meaning it is charming and manly to run after female colleagues. And questions about journalists not doing their job, because they do not reveal relevant information about powerful men.

Now, that is what I call positive effects of the DSK affair! All these questions and debates are needed. They bring light into rooms that have been in the dark for too long.

The DSK affair is a painful one, for all parties. It is however bringing some very healthy debates, and I hope these debates materialize into better working environments for women in France. I have a suspicion that many women are used to *the way things are around here*, and that stories like these create an "Aha! it doesn't have to be like this!"

*

This DSK story showed that a big event made people wake up, and it got some focus on the sexual harassment and objectification that many women experience in France. But, still, things don't change from one day to the other, and I think that many people are like a "Frog in the Pot".

Frogs, People and Hot Water

If you have done some kind of stress training or heard of how we react to stress, you may have come across the story about *The Frog in the Pot*. Quick summary: if you put a frog in very hot water, he will jump out, but if you put him in cold water and slowly warm it up, he will not realise it and actually get cooked.. Not a very nice story, but it does illustrate very clearly what happens to us when we "turn up the heat" at work and slowly get used to the stress until it has gone way too far.

Other than coping (or not) with stress, I think there are many other situations where *we stay in the warm water* and fail to react. As mentioned in the story about DSK, some women seem to have gotten used to being discriminated against and don't notice it anymore, like when they get remarks about their looks all day.

One weekend at our holiday house I was surprised by a woman in her early thirties. We were two couples who met a retired man. We stopped to talk, and this man shook hands with the men and talked with the men. He did not shake hands or nod to us, the women, nor did he address us while talking. I later asked the other woman what she thought of that and she said she hadn't noticed! But since I mentioned it, she found the behaviour to be rather odd. I thought it was rather odd that she didn't notice, especially at her age! Warm water…

*

When discussing gender differences and different expectations, there are many similarities across the world. However, having a foot in both Norway and France (north and south Europe), I also see that not all is the same. The following blog is a reflection on the discussions I saw going on in Norway in 2011 from the outside.

Dance a New Dance?

It is with curiosity that I follow current discussions on gender in the Norwegian media. Having lived abroad since 2004 and worked internationally for more than a decade, my day-to-day life is not the same as other Norwegian women. And therefore I particularly like to know what happens back in the motherland, the country famous for its egalitarianism and the first country to implement quotas to get more women on company boards.

There is a long tradition in Norway of focusing on women's right to equal pay and access to senior roles in corporate and governments. Only Iceland has a higher proportion of women in work than Norway, with seven out of ten women at work (compared to eight out of ten men). In 1913, Norway was the first sovereign state to grant women the right to vote (men were granted the right to vote in 1898). According to the World Economic Forum (WEF), Norway ranks 2nd in the world on the Gender Gap Index (Iceland ranks 1st). (2014 numbers, Norway is down to 3rd)

But still... Recent studies show that Norwegian women still choose fairly traditionally; they are highly represented in the less-paid public sector in jobs like nursing and teaching. And many work part-time - which proves to be a block when it comes to getting to higher positions. According to a report by Catherine Hakim at the London School of Economics, countries like the USA (a country that offers no paid maternity leave), have more success in getting women up into the ranks in corporate and governments. And this is what kicked off a discussion in the Norwegian media in 2011.

The discussion is rather vivid around *what matters*; building a healthy and happy family or making a career and building pension points? Some have argued that it is a responsibility for women to work full-time and make the country's wheels go around (Norway has an unemployment rate of around 3%, which means there is a lack of labour in certain industries). The phrase *personal choice* is often brought up, that the women chose to focus on family values. Combining work and family is seen to be a real challenge, as having domestic help is not very common. Some people say; *women need to choose like men, men have to participate more at home and our social benefits take the mothers away from the work scene for too long.* Others say: *we have real freedom to choose what we*

want, and we want children AND work, women have more talent for jobs in the caring industry.

I think three factors influence the current *state of the nation:*

1 - *Culture*. In Norway it is not as common as in many other countries to hire full-time nannies and house-cleaners. This may be due to a non-hierarchical structure and the importance of everyone being equal. Hiring domestic help feels uncomfortable to many as this could give a feeling of being in a 'master/servant' situation. Even though the domestic work is fairly evenly shared between the man and the woman, it is still the women who feel responsible for shopping and cleaning and taking care of the family (one could argue that she could let go a bit more..). Some years ago there was an article in the Norwegian financial magazine *Hegnar* that pointed out the fact that even though there are less women working in France for example, those who do, get to higher and more powerful positions. This article also pointed out that women have to choose: they cannot be powerful leaders, caring mothers who cook all the meals, and attend all school events - and being a magnificent wife. Choices and prioritizations have to be made, and it appears that Norwegian women still want to do it all - but they see it is not possible. Result: part-time job.

2 - *Society*. On the subject of 'freedom to choose', I am not so sure... Even with years of trying to make men and women choose non-traditional careers for their gender, there are still ideas about what is 'a girl thing to do' and 'a boy thing to do'. I participated in a discussion online, making this point, and a friend of mine came back to me with an example. She told me that she was very surprised to hear all the reactions about her son having started to dance ballet: "Isn't that for girls?" After having had several negative reactions from the fathers picking up their daughters, her son didn't want to go anymore. Now, shouldn't girls and boys have the freedom to choose whatever they want without getting any comments about it? So, my point is that within the society we live in, even in places like Norway even today, people still possess ideas about what girls and boys should choose when it comes to activities which are 'correct' for their gender. I believe this subconsciously steers us and the career choices we make.

3 - *Communication*. Through what I have read in the news online, I get the sense that Norwegian men are tired. Tired of the focus on women, tired of hearing that women 'hit the glass ceiling', tired of hearing they are not helping enough at home and with the children, tired of not feeling listened to in matters of sharing the children in a divorce and tired of not feeling appreciated for the changes they have done. Maybe the focus needs to

change in Norway? More of women *and* men's rights? This is already a dialogue, but how can the dialogue be improved..?

Generally speaking, there is a change going on among the gender specialists and diversity champions in Europe and the US. They're saying it's important to stop talking about *rising women and falling men*. The trend is towards the perspective that we need men and companies to embrace the shift in women, not fear it. To meet halfway, and dance a new dance. Both men and women have their role to play here.

*

My friend's story about her son meeting negative reactions because he wanted to dance ballet, made me think of how colour-coded we have become. Pink for girls, blue for boys. Interestingly enough, in the early 1900s pink was a colour for boys, it was considered too *strong* or too *flashy* for women. This changed after Word War II, and reached an all time high in the 1980s with the fashion for pastels. When I was a girl of about 10-12 years-old I was puzzled at why most of the girls at school decorated their bedrooms in pink. As mentioned above, I wasn't particularly fond of the colour (didn't go well with my childhood red hair!) and I didn't understand why we should all have the same decoration.

Some 35 years later, we are more colour- and gender-coded than ever. A newspaper discussion in Norway in 2013 stated that parents who want practical clothes for their young daughters, need to go to the boys' section in the clothing stores. Professors argue that, with the clothes available for girls, they can only remain still in the schoolyard, it does not encourage play and movement. They lose out on healthy exercise, but not only that; a lot is learnt in physical play - being part of a team, getting up again after having lost, still being friends after having lost a game. All this is valuable preparation for adult life.

Back to the more international arena - women across the world are increasingly attracted to being their own boss, myself included. The following article reflects that trend.

A New Era of Women Entrepreneurs?

(Published in *Diversity Journal* April 24 2012) "Female entrepreneurs currently account for approximately a third of all entrepreneurs worldwide, and the U.S. Census Bureau predicts that by the year 2025, the share of women entrepreneurship in that country will increase to more than 55 per cent." *The Global Legal Post,* April 2012.

As a female entrepreneur, my eyes are always open to anything to do with the subject of female entrepreneurship, and there is a lot out there! Late last year there was a comment in a Norwegian newspaper about "why do so many women run away from companies to become entrepreneurs" and a few days later I found an interview on an American site asking two successful lady business owners "why aren't there more women entrepreneurs?". Two rather different angles in two different countries, but both indicated an interest in this subject.

Women are considered to be risk-averse. Yet according to a study quoted in BBC News in February 2011, "Compared with men, women were found to aspire more to running their own company than achieving higher rank within a firm." According to the same news channel in 2008, "Women are twice as likely as their male counterparts to set up businesses following big life changes such as ill-health, divorce or moving house." Across the world, we see more and more women starting up business, but the bottom-line is, there are more men than women entrepreneurs. (Figure on the next page shows data drawn from OECD on percentages of female self-employment, year 2000 compared to 2010.)

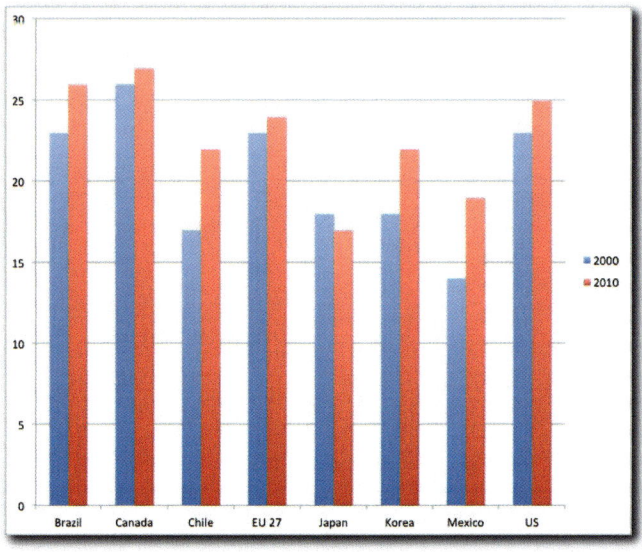

Women are also supposed to have less self-confidence and less experience in self-promotion than men, and I tend to agree - considering my experience as an HR professional, coach, and member of women's networks. This isn't an advantage when being self-employed. You need lots of resilience and courage - and a good dose of self-confidence to keep going. Despite the struggle, women entrepreneurs have enough motivation and drive to shut down the inner negative voices and go for it anyway.

So what attracts the women that are not risk-averse to get into this new territory? Or are they still risk-averse, but there are other attractions? Speaking for myself, I was attracted to choosing my tasks, or 'following my passion'. I was attracted to working with several clients as opposed to working in one corporate culture. I was also attracted to making my own decisions, without going through an authorization process to implement an idea. In my case, I do take calculated risks from time to time. Talking with other women, words like "freedom" and "flexibility" do tend to pop up.

In developing countries, support is given to women entrepreneurs as they are more likely to return the money they borrow and the whole family benefit from the income.

I have read in various media that women today are more attracted to starting up a business due to the lack of flexibility with their employer and also hitting the 'glass ceiling' or the 'sticky floor. Despite the challenges already mentioned (risk aversion and lack of self confidence), more and more women feel drawn towards being their own boss. It is possibly due to the various options of help now available. Here's what I've found on that point:

- Numerous books; examples being *100 Ways To Boost Your Self-Confidence: Believe in Yourself and Others Will Too* and *Self-Promotion and the Making of a Brand* and *How to Start and Run Your Home-based Business*.
- Companies that sell 'how to set up businesses' (financials, bureaucracy, law, sales, how to grow business, etc.) Some of them focus on women entrepreneurs only.
- Coaching. This is particularly helpful on the personal side of setting up a business, for example self-confidence. A coaching tip: find an image, a symbol, a saying or draw a picture that inspires you every day and place it where you can see it all the time.
- Women's network meetings for entrepreneurs. The Professional Women's Network (PWN) arranges information meetings for entrepreneurs and there are special clubs for women entrepreneurs.
- Individual effort. Entrepreneurs can come together on an individual basis to give each other support. Meeting other female entrepreneurs over lunch to discuss deeper challenges and get advice can be inspiring and motivating. Often there is much in common and the entrepreneurs coach each other on challenges, fears and hang-ups. Knowing that you are not alone in having them - even if 'others' look so successful and 'knowing it all' - is motivation to keep going.

So, are we moving into a new era of women entrepreneurs? The overall trend seems to indicate that. The trend may be speeding up as we are finding more and more role models and a supportive infrastructure for women. This may have a positive spin-off effect on medium to large enterprises: how do you keep your female talent happy so that they don't leave you for a solo career?

*

I have mentioned societal pressure on and expectations of women a few times. One of these is to look good. There are slight cultural differences on how important it is, and in general women have more pressure than men in this regard. I believe this dates back to the time when women had to *marry well* as they could not provide for themselves. Various information in newspapers, social media and TED Talks, some of it in connection with International Women's Day, triggered me to write the following two blogs.

Cosmetic Surgery, Freedom and Women

A friend of mine posted an article from the *Miami Herald* on Facebook about an 18-year old girl who became completely handicapped after an accident during cosmetic surgery. A young, beautiful woman, who wanted to be even more beautiful, is now brain-damaged.

On Facebook, the discussion went in many directions. Who is to blame? Parents, the girl herself, doctors with no ethics? I would like to ask the question: why has cosmetic surgery become such a huge industry in the first place? I will focus on women, as the majority of people having cosmetic surgery are women. And I will zoom in on those who don't really need it - they have had no accidents nor been born with birth defects.

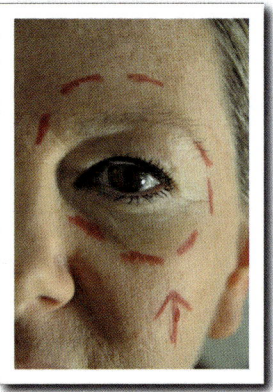

Historically, women were dependent on *marrying well*, since they had less opportunities to get a job and provide for their own lives. It is still the case in several parts of the world. To find a future (wealthy) husband, your chances were, and are, better if you are very beautiful. As cosmetic surgery has become more affordable, those who want/need to marry well have more access to becoming even more attractive. It is understandable that the more you see marriage as the only way to live or get wealthy, the more you will be drawn to cosmetic surgery. However, in many parts of the world, women can now provide for themselves, and also become rich and successful, so there is no real practical need, as we have freedom to live our lives pretty much as we wish to.

Then the question becomes: why take such a risk, just to be slightly more beautiful - when you don't have to? The answer could be pressure from society, or role models from movies, music videos and magazines or convinced she will be happier with an 'improved exterior'. Okay, but why listen? Why do some listen and others not? I know of several parents that pay for cosmetic surgery on their children, because they think they are 'helping them' feel better. The examples I have in mind are beautiful girls that don't need 'help'... What are these parents teaching their children about values? That we don't care about the inner person as much as their outer image and appearance?

Clearly, there is big money to be earned as a cosmetic surgeon and there are also many insecure women out there (I will hint about how we are raised influences this). Some clinics use this insecurity in a calculated way and create a need where there isn't one.

I recently read an article where the author claimed; *body focus is the new religion*. He meant that we have lost our interest for spirituality and interior growth; instead we spend our time building up perfect exteriors. Interestingly enough, studies have shown that there are more suicides among women who have had breast surgery. Life doesn't miraculously change after acquiring new and 'better' breasts.

In my part of the world, women wearing hijab, niqab and burka are looked upon with suspicion. I am personally not in favour of covering up women's faces, but what 'freedom' are we talking about when women think they have to look like models (and show as much skin as possible) - a perfect image that doesn't even exist?

I have more questions than answers, but I find it sad that cosmetic surgery is becoming so *normal*. Unfortunately, reality is that even in the business world, more attractive people get better paid and are offered more promotions... I wish for a world where parents teach that inner qualities are valued, that we are judged on who we are and what we contribute - not what we look like, and that society embraces diversity rather than clones.

Stereotyping and Unconscious Bias Caused by Advertisements

Around International Women's Day (8 March) there is usually heightened attention in the news about the situation of women and their progress, as well as current challenges across the world. Two videos came my way that impressed me. One was a 45-min video by Jean Kilbourne called *Killing us Softly* and the other was a 13-min video on TEDx by Caroline Hedman. Both highlight the objectification of women - and men - in the media.

What is objectification? Roughly speaking it means that a person's worth or role in society is reduced to an instrument of something or a thing/an object. According to Caroline Hedman we see this in advertisements when only parts of a body are shown, or the person is a stand-in for an object, the person is being violated or integrity is violated, her sexual availability is her defining characteristics, the person is interchangeable/can be swopped by anyone or the person is a commodity - can be bought or sold.

Objectification has a 'price'. According to studies, these are the effects for women:
- Depression - Eating disorders
- Sexual dysfunction - Body shame
- Female competition - No power - Lower self-esteeem

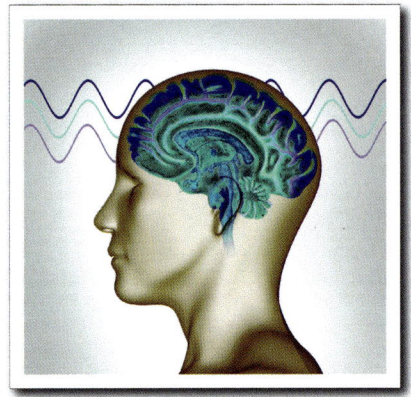

I am aware of the media's use of stereotyped images and the objectification of women in particular, but seeing these videos I was shocked by the mere masses of messages we are hit by and how it influences children and teenagers. They are basically made to believe in something which doesn't exist; models that are computer images, not real women. Or catwalk models who die from anorexia. And it becomes international; the white, thin, blond, blue-eyed woman is the role model across the world - which basically means there is no chance whatsoever for most women on this planet to look like that. What does that do to young women's self-confidence? No good at all. The various advertisements tell you that as a woman you are not worth anything unless you are pretty, so you better run to get some cosmetic surgery! Men are also increasingly feeling this pressure, but not as massively as women.

Children and teenagers are more vulnerable to these images, but we are all bombarded by media everywhere we move, it is therefore only logical that we become influenced by it somehow. Some more, some less, but according to the studies made by Kilbourne and Hedman separately it is probably *more*, as the cosmetic surgery business is flourishing.

What worries me the most is the stereotyped images of women being passive, sexualized, objectified - having something done to them. I do beleive it sneaks up on us and becomes an unconscious bias regarding women's role in society. Men are most of the time shown in more realistic positions, showing strength. Not particularly helpful images for women who want to succeed at work. Several of the advertisements glorify violence, and often by men to women. Considering a world-wide problem of violence against women, I think we as consumers should speak up. Enough already!

*

The subjects of cosmetic surgery and objectification make me think about beauty in the workplace. Being beautiful is an advantage for both men and women, I have seen several studies on how beautiful people get the better jobs and are paid more than those who are not. When we bring age into the picture, however, the advantages change whether you are a man or a woman. A beautiful female leader I talked with when I lived in the USA, confided in me that she could notice a great difference after turning 50. She was aware that through life she had sometimes received special treatment and favours, but as her beauty faded, so did the special treatment and she started to feel *invisible*.

I will end this chapter with a blog about stress, which is both a male and a female problem. However, in Europe there is higher percentage of sick leave among women, and more cases of depression - alas there is a difference. In general, women still do more housework and take care of the children, on top of their job. This picture is changing, however, especially in the Nordic countries.

Women and Serenity, or rather, Lack of

I'm sure you have heard your friends and colleagues talk about their busy lives; busy at work, busy with kids (having to bring them everywhere), busy social activities, busy taking care of elderly parents, busy preparing gourmet dinners... Sound familiar? Maybe not only friends and colleagues, what about your own reality?

In the spring of 2014 I delivered a workshop for the local Professional Women's Network (PWN) on *Burnout: Warning Signals and Coping Strategies*. Of the 16 women who attended, most recognized this excessive busy-ness, and the majority had experienced deep levels of stress or a burnout of some degree.

We are challenged by wanting to perform in all areas of life; in the workplace, at home, with friends and wider family, and personally (for example sports). Women tend to be 'worse' than men, wanting perfection and putting very high expectations on themselves in many arenas. But, in the long run, it doesn't work, there has to be slack somewhere. Women in Europe have a higher percentage of sick leave than men (in certain countries as much as 80% more than men!), so something has to change.

One arena that could implement change is the *workplace*. Some companies have understood the importance of creativity, and that overworked employees are not creative. For example one business expects; "IF YOU CANNOT FIGURE OUT HOW TO DO YOUR JOB IN 40 HOURS, WE WILL FIRE YOU." (Quote from article on Fastcompany.com: *Why you need to stop bragging about how busy you are*)

Another arena is *our heads*. Be conscious that we have a choice. Choose your employer, or how you want to respond to conditions at your workplace. Prioritize; what needs to be done, what is a nice-to-do; *do I need this to be perfect or not?* In my workshop the participants had several suggestions as to how one can manage life better and avoid the feeling of overload:

- Remember what is important
- Meditation
- A good laugh
- Keep things in perspective
- Setting limits
- Time off; self-time
- Celebrate

The last point is important, yet often forgotten; celebrate our successes, and celebrate what goes well, be grateful for the little (and big) things in life. This contributes to positive thinking and good mental health. Good mental health has an impact on good physical health. On that point, there has been a study done at the University of Wisconsin-Madison, called the National Health Interview Survey (NHIS). They interviewed 30,000 adults in the U.S.

over an eight-year period. Participants were asked how much stress they'd experienced in the previous year, and if they believed that stress was harmful to their health. Public death records were used to find out who died over the eight-year period. The interesting results were;

- o People who experienced a lot of stress had a 43 percent higher risk of dying-but only if they also believed that stress was harmful to them.
- o People who experienced a lot of stress but did not view stress as harmful were no more likely to die. In fact, they had a lower risk of dying than anyone else in the study-even people with relatively little stress.

Conclusion: How you think about stress matters. When you change your mind about stress, you can change your body's response to stress.

Do you want a more serene life? Get out of the *I'm so busy* trend! I think we can start with ourselves. If you suffer from too much 'busy-ness', consider what matters to you. Make baby step changes in the direction you want to go. Communicate to others what matters to you. If enough people do just that, it will have an impact on their surroundings.

Final remarks

How do we focus on gender equality without anyone feeling judged or blamed? I have heard several men and women say that they believe they do what they can to include and promote everyone, but that it is not being appreciated or that it is not seen. Others feel they are being blamed for historical injustice. This can lead to a feeling of resistance and demotivation as a result of the D&I specialist telling them what to do or what to change.

Status quo is that there is a misrepresentation of the population when it comes to female leaders (figure with data drawn from the EU Commission on women and men on boards in EU, October 2014).

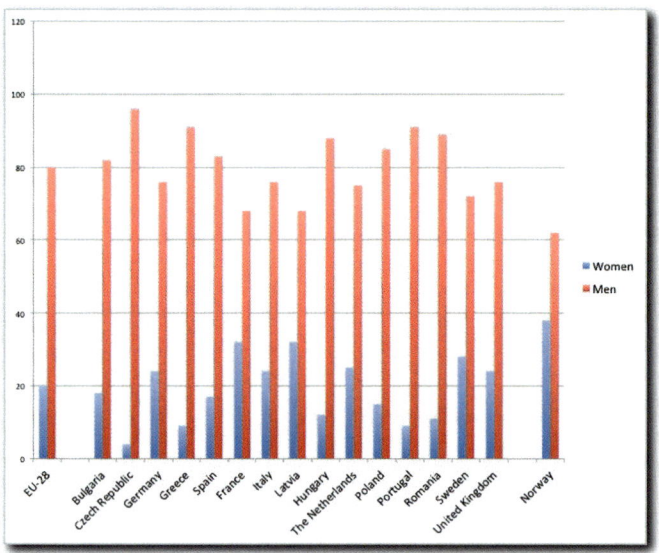

Women still experience objectification. Men and women are coloured by stereotypes and traditions, it is not always easy to judge whether we have real freedom to choose or freedom to be authentic. It is not a given that a man can take paternity leave or embrace his 'soft side'. Change is still needed in the area of gender equality but change will happen. I believe we can get that through resilience and creativity, let things mature and repeat the resilience and creativity. During this process it is an advantage to stay open-minded and listen, whether a man or a woman. Walk in the other person's shoes, see the world from that person's perspective. (Many a male leader has noticed injustice in the work place when his daughter started working.)

In Autumn 2014 the UN started the campaign #HeForShe, highlighted by the speech of the young actress Emma Watson. She refers to the inequality that still exists and the trend that the word *feminism* has become negative, associated with advantages for women and hate of men. Among the feminists, some have started using the words *human rights* instead, to create a more constructive dialogue. The UN video has received a lot of positive attention, and there are domino-effects with for example male politicians wearing t-shirts with the text *I'm a feminist*.

Feminist or *humanist*, whatever we label it, the world would benefit from fair treatment of both men and women, giving them all possible opportunities to reach their potential and live their *dream* (as mentioned in the following chapter on Generations). *What can you do to encourage fair treatment for women and men around you?*

Maybe one day we'll live to see a non-white nun as a pope.

CHAPTER SIX:
GENERATIONS OR CHANGING TIMES

There are several 'young' generations in the workplace right now, categorised in X and Y (and Z) generations. These young, or fairly young, people are high-tech, multitaskers, and often quite demanding. According to studies, many want work with a meaning, in fact "meaning and purpose" is often the number one reason for accepting a job offer. Research done by various organisations (for example CatchAFire, Deloitte, or Accenture) indicates that the majority of Generation Y seek to work at companies that are socially responsible. They do not readily accept a manager's authority if he or she does not show the necessary skills of a manager. They move jobs quicker than previous generations.

We are in a time of transformation, that influences many generations, and seen from a diversity perspective I think it creates lots of changes, challenges and opportunities.

The few blogs that follow are focused on the influence the younger generation have on all of us, as well as a positive focus on aging. There is a descriptive overview of the different generations at the end of this chapter.

Zapping Lives

Although I'm specialised in the fields of Diversity & Inclusion and Coaching, I still read about my former profession; Talent and Recruitment. In this field, the subject of the *new generation* often comes up, in the contexts of how to understand them, what they need, what motivates them, etc. One of the characteristics of Generation Y, also called the *Harry Potter Generation*, is a strong capability in new technology, communications and media - and that they constantly zap from one thing to the other.

I have read that there is some discussion to when *Generation Y* calculation starts, but roughly speaking we talk about people born mid/late 1970's to late 1990's. This is a generation that has had access to technology like never before; mobile phones, home computers, social media, virtual chatting, internet shopping and virtual games like Second Life. It is not uncommon that a member of the Harry Potter generation listens to her Ipod while she does her homework on the Mac at the same time as she chats on her Ipad, with the TV on in the background... (We are talking about the rich western part of the world, of course.) Naturally trained multitaskers!

The flipside to all the multitasking, according to research, is that the capability to focus on something for a longer period of time is underdeveloped. But do we need to focus anymore? And is Generation Y the only zapping, multitasking generation?

Honestly, I think anyone has to be a multitasking zapper these days! More or less. Technology has brought us so many possibilities to connect and do several things at the same time, and we have become so incredibly accessible with our Blackberrys and Iphones, Mac-Lights and Ipads. The 'Harry Potter's' have the advantage by having grown up with it, but most people have to deal with it at some point. Whether you are comfortable with it or not depends on your interests, capabilities, and appetite for new learning.

And do we really need to focus on one thing for a longer time? I must admit that I have become such a zapper that I have trouble focusing myself! But yes, I do need to focus and I think we all need to at times. To read a business book. To concentrate in a webinar (without reading email or do paper filing) or in a meeting. To be present with clients. (To be present with anyone, really). To really talk with and listen to the children, and spouse (shut off the TV while having dinner!!) To slow down and listen to ourselves... And by that I mean for example listen to the signals the body gives when being tired instead of running over the feeling by having more coffee, more activity, more zapping.

Regarding *being present* or *mindful,* I talked with an old man who lives on the same street as I about how we had spent Christmas. He told me that he and his wife had Christmas lunch with their children and extended family, twelve people altogether, and many of them had their smartphones with them at the table, always checking messages or looking for something on their phones. He didn't like it at all, and certainly wasn't sure of their mental presence.

Probably as a result of the multi-tasking or noisy times we live in, many people find balance in focusing on *mindfulness.* Mindfulness and mindfulness techniques help us to get grounded again. One company I read about hired a mindfulness coach in a customer service centre, and their customer satisfaction went up dramatically. Additionally, the employees reported back higher motivation and satisfaction at work. Sitting in an open space office may at times be challenging and one needs the ability to concentrate and focus despite the animation around you. In case you have not heard about mindfulness, I have added an explanation from Wikipedia at the end of this chapter.

Zapping lives are busy lives which can be fun and energetic one. And that's great, as long as we are able to find the right balance, the balance that works for us each individually. The balance of *doing* versus *being,* the balance of *ying* and *yang,* the *rule of opposites;* whatever resonates with you.

*

Many of these *advanced zappers* have high computer literacy, as they have had access to this technology all their lives. So, it's easy for them: an example is to be seen from one of the stories from French national Sebastien, 24 years-old. Sebastien has recently finished his Master's in Marketing and Business strategies, and has just started a job in Marketing in the United States.

"As an integral part of my Master's I worked in a large enterprise in Paris. I soon discovered that what I consider to be a basic level of computer understanding, or even basic use of Excel, is not always the case for my older colleagues. One time I produced a work sheet that would give us easy access to useful information, faster than before. However, my colleagues didn't take advantage of this tool, because they didn't understand how to use it. I was surprised, it really wasn't that complicated and the return of investment was clearly there.

"Something I also noticed right away was the practice of wearing a suit and tie - even though we did not meet with clients. I was wondering why we dressed up for the computer screen! Once a week we had 'casual Friday', the day that everyone could wear jeans. I didn't see any difference in the work performance when wearing casual clothes...

"In my free time I helped for about 6 months with an international project that was targeting people in Europe through social media. I realized that although we spoke the same language, all of us didn't have the same vocabulary. One person, in his 40s, was clearly not up to speed on words that are commonly used in social media. It meant we had to explain more, it took longer to discuss."

*

The Generation Y is also considered to be more focused on meaningful work and having the attitude *work to live* as opposed *to live to work*, something that appeals to me personally. The blog that follows is inspired of this thinking.

Work Less, Earn More?

I received an advertisement in my inbox about an eBook that will teach you to work less and earn more. Sounds like a dream!

I have seen similar titles lately from various consultants selling coaching and training in different formats. It must be a trend or a signal, maybe; "we're tired of the old models, here's a new way of managing your life". Maybe the new generation is influencing the older one? The generation that believes in working for a purpose and/or enjoyment, not living to work.

About four years ago I talked with a coach in a seminar who told me "the work-yourself-to-death-attitude is not necessary, we can work reasonable hours and live a good life". She shared her own story with me, how she had managed to create the life she wanted; a life with interesting work, decent pay and time for her family and friends and hobbies. Her story made an impression on me. My surroundings (including media) have told me, and still tell me, that you have to work "non-stop" to be successful and have a pleasant life moneywise. You have to be active, a go-getter! Especially if you are an entrepreneur...

So, isn't it true anymore?? Is there another way?

Whenever I go to Norway I'm amazed when seeing the traffic jams in early afternoon. People work seven and a half hours per day and respect that timing (there are always exceptions, and some people bring their laptops home, but I'm talking in general terms). They have nice houses and nice cars and they have all afternoon and evening to do other things than work - those with a family are probably playing taxi driver for the kids... When I see that, I'm thinking "I must have misunderstood something". I have the house and the car, but I didn't have the time during large parts of my adult life - and I still don't - compared to the 'Norwegian way'. So, I must admit that this advertisement this morning spoke to me... Is it really possible? I guess I should just try one of these workshops/seminars or buy that eBook!

*

From the young generation's influence to the wish for staying young... We do have lots of pressures on the physical side of 'looking young', but also mentally; 'be dynamic', be 'up to speed'. However, with the demographics changing, it is highly likely that the western world's work force in the future will be older. This due to declining birth rates, a certain level of mismatch of studies taken and jobs available, and last, but not least, the high unemployment rates among young people in many European countries for the last few years mean that many have lost out on valuable years of acquiring job experience. ("Youth will become a lost generation if they do not acquire at a young age the relevant skills, jobs in which they can use these skills and earnings with which they can live and lead a self-determined life," ILO's economists write in the 2011 report Jobs, growth and social justice.) Having worked as a recruiter and an HR Manager, I clearly see the need for 'mature' talents, and have not been happy about what seemed to be a general skewed view on hiring staff in a certain age group.

The article below is inspired by a study that was done about happiness. Apparently we get happier with age, an even better argument to hire mature staff - they will bring a good ambience!

Generations and Happiness

(Published in *Diversity Journal* June 20, 2013) In the western world on average we live longer, look younger, and have children later. The media talk about "Fifty being the new forty" - meaning people behave, dress, and look younger than before. The fact that we live longer actually creates challenges for governments - how to pay for retirement when people need it for so much longer? In France the solution in 2012 was to increase the retirement age. France is not the only country taking action, or considering doing so. Government rules or not, some people choose to work longer than they have to, as they feel fit and they love their jobs. Others look forward to a long 'second life' at leisure.

A while back I attended a workshop run by a 72-year-old man who kept saying that "life only gets better." He referred to research published in *The Economist's* December 2010 issue, 'The U-bend of Life,' which shows people only get happier and happier after the peak of unhappiness at the age of forty-six. This factor is influenced by gender, personality, external circumstances, and age. Some examples: women tend to be happier than men (but also more depressed). Educated people are happier, as long as their investment gives them a good income. At older ages we tend to have more money (less worry about paying bills) and the children are out of the house (less anxiety).

Everyone is aware that optimists generally enjoy better health and live longer than pessimists. This means people's attitudes are important. But can attitude be changed? Or can pessimists learn to be optimists? Can you learn to see the glass half full instead of half empty?

My assumption is that many people would say we cannot change personality. From my experience as a professional coach, I would argue that you can alter some aspects of your personality, for instance there are exercises you can do to focus more on positive parts of your life. By implementing a new habit, you actually do see results - people tend to open their eyes to what works well in their life and what they have already achieved, as well as noticing 'little wonders' around them. There is some interesting research done on *positive psychology* that shows positivity can be learned and change can be made, specifically Carole Kauffmann's *Positive Psychology: The Science at the Heart of Coaching*.

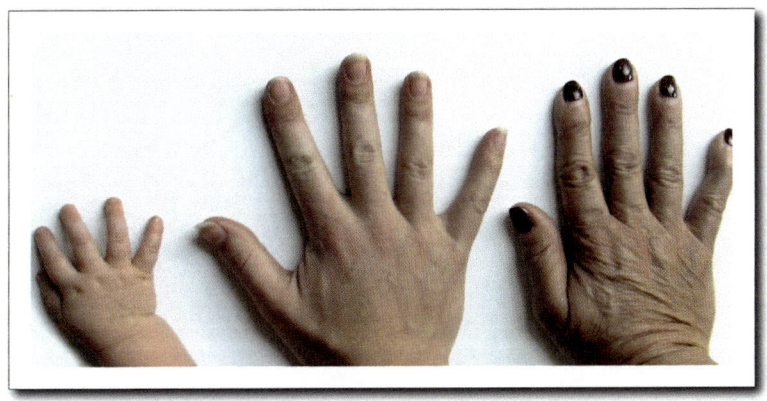

I wonder whether the research presented in *The Economist* would alter over time, considering that Generation Y (people born between 1980 and 2000) seek fun as well as meaning in their workplace and want both work/life balance and personal development. Wouldn't this have an impact on their stress levels or unhappiness at a young age, for example, if they achieve work/life balance in their thirties? How much time would it take for the work environment to change with the wishes of the Generation Ys, or will it ever happen? Only time will tell.

Looked at from a diversity angle I think Generation Y attitudes create opportunity for positive change and new, positive ways of working.

Thus, my key take-aways are:
a) Research shows that you get happier with age.
b) If you work on seeing the good in life, you can become even more positive - and thereby live longer.

c) Generation Y work attitudes may influence their feeling of happiness at a younger age.
d) The future looks bright...

*

You might have come across this quote (from unknown): "When I was 5 years old, my mom always told me that happiness was the key to life. When I went to school, they asked me what I wanted to be when I grew up. I wrote down happy. They told me I didn't understand the assignment and I told them they didn't understand life."

From happiness with age to a blog on career choices that young, and not so young, people need to make. Different generations have received different advice on what is the right thing to choose. A challenge I hear today is that there are too many choices! There are less limitations, the world is open, and it can therefore be difficult to know which profession is the best fit. An interesting situation in Norway these days is that the economy is so strong that students have money to keep moving from one study to the other. The blog that follows might make you philosophise; "What is my dream, in career and generally in life?"

Living the Dream

When I was a teenager in the early 80s we were recommended to educate ourselves towards jobs where there was a demand - something that would secure you a job. I didn't hear "what are your interests" or "where do you excel at school?" Still, we had more choice than the previous generation, as I grew up in a time where everyone had the possibility of extending their education beyond the obligatory nine years. Today, I hear many people advise the young to follow their passions, or to aim for an area where they can use their strengths. I also think there is more openness towards following an artistic career in music, movies, writing, etc. Probably because there are many role models of people who are successful in these areas.

I wonder, though, how the economic situation in Southern Europe will impact choices young people take these days?

As a career coach I see that people in their early 40s (some early 30s) would like to do something else professionally. They feel they have been sidetracked, or they have not followed their interests and passions. Looking ahead, they cannot imagine staying in the same job or field. But changing path is scary, plus it means hard work, possibly also going back to school. The upside is that with experience, one quickly adds value even if it is a new profession.

I come across a fair number of people who 'jump off' the traditional career path and follow their dreams: working as a clairvoyant, building a retreat in an exotic area of the world, opening a refuge for badly treated animals, doing voluntary work, becoming a coach, teacher, etc., etc. What I see that they have in common, is that they are drawn towards *jobs with meaning*, which could be a reaction to having worked in the cold and cynical business-world (pardon the cliché). There might be an influence by the younger generation; the generation that believes in working for a purpose and/or enjoyment, not living to work.

My mother told me a story about a man she had seen when she was young. "He was polishing shoes and had done so most of his life. He always looked so happy and one time I asked him why. He answered: I have a wonderful life. I can do my work while I think about what my next painting will look like or how I can improve the one I am working on. And I meet a lot of nice people, too". It made an impact on my mother, realizing how one can find pleasure in what seemingly is a boring job.

Back to *living the dream*, it doesn't necessarily mean that you have found your dream job, it can also mean that you have the possibility to spend time on your favourite hobby and you have created a life around you that you dreamed of as a child. Taking this a step further, living the dream is also to realize and notice all the riches you have in your life; for example good health, good husband/wife, a nice place to live, good friends, good colleagues, good relations with family, a beautiful view ... - and being aware that having food on the table, a roof over your head, a job, and absence of war and violence are luxuries for a large majority on this planet.

I would argue that, at any age, we are better off following our interests and passions. I believe we do a better job at work, and are of more joy to people around us. A win-win at work and home. It may not be easy to do, but in my opinion, worth the price!

Final remarks

I think that the younger generations bring several positive aspects to work life. If I could generalize, I would say that they appear to be naturally embracing of diversity, as many of them have grown up with a more multicultural society than the generations before them. They want life to be a balance of fun and work, which seems to be a healthy approach, if you ask me. What I sometimes struggle with, is a somewhat lack of persistence if things are difficult, giving up rather quickly. I have delivered workshops on how to understand the preferences of the four-five generations that are currently in the work place, and there are clearly challenges when it comes to bridging understanding of the various values.

I read an article about the Millennials (Generation Y), describing the attitude "they think they should be rewarded for showing up at work". I mentioned this in a workshop and it really made people laugh! They recognised it 100% and talked about the additional task in training young employees not only the job, but also general good behaviour.

As you have seen from Sebastien's stories, the other side of the coin is that young people ask questions ("Why do we dress up in suits when we don't meet any clients"). This is not special for this particular generation, but it's another example of why diversity of generations is useful in the workplace.

To close this chapter out, here is a brief overview from various articles of the current generations in the workplace and their values. (Yes, we are more than just our generation, but you might be surprised in seeing how much this resonates)

Traditionalists/Veterans/Silent Generation (1922-1945). Mostly retired, but not all.
- Duty before pleasure
- Respect for authority, adhere to rules

- o Responsibility, conformity
- o Giving back is important

Baby Boomers/Me Generation/Sandwich Generation (1946-1964)
- o Equal rights, equal opportunities
- o Personal growth, personal gratification
- o Optimism, anything is possible
- o Question everything

Generation X/Baby Bust (1965-1980)
- o Entrepreneurial, independent
- o High job expectations, lack of organizational loyalty
- o Suspicious of Boomer values, informal
- o Think globally, diversity

Generation Y/Millennials (1981-2000)
- o Avid consumers, extreme fun
- o Confidence, sociability, most educated generation
- o Optimism and street smarts
- o Highly tolerant, diversity, members of global community

Generation Z (2001 -) are starting to be seen in school work-placements. They will be the most socially networked generation in history.

What do you recognise? What are your own challenges with working with other generations? What would make it a learning experience?

*Mindfulness; information drawn from Wikipedia.

- o There is the spiritual version; "a spiritual or psychological faculty (indriya) that, according to the teaching of the Buddha, is considered to be of great importance in the path to enlightenment. It is one of *the seven factors of enlightenment*".

- o Or the psychological version; "is the focusing of attention and awareness, based on the concept of mindfulness in Buddhist meditation, but is defined in many ways. (...) Despite its roots in Buddhism, mindfulness is not inherently religious and is often taught independent of religion. (...) Research suggests that mindfulness practices are useful in the treatment of pain, stress, anxiety, depressive relapse, eating disorders, and addiction."

- And then there is mindfulness cognitive therapy, mindfulness breathing, mindfulness meditation and mindfulness coaching, even mindfulness leadership *(fitness for the mind)*.

In short, how I understand it, is that mindfulness is the capability of *being present in the now*, the opposite of *zapping* from one activity to another. And this helps us to produce better work and be a better manager/friend/spouse/parent, etc.

CHAPTER SEVEN:
NO DIVERSITY WITHOUT INCLUSION

We humans have a tendency to create in- and out-groups, as children and adults. The in-group, or insiders, are *people like us*. The out-group, or outsiders, are *people like them*. People in the in-group are often seen as individuals, whereas people in the out-group are often seen as representatives of a group; "They do this"/"they are like that". It is never a good feeling to know you are in the out-group, and in a business environment it is creating an ambience that is not getting the best out of its people. People work best and are happy to go to work if they feel included, listened to and that they have the same chances as everyone else.

Being in a minority or majority can also give a sense of in- or out-group, but it is not the same. A minority group might be in power (such as people of European descent in previous apartheid South-Africa), therefore the in-group. And a minority might be out of power, or in the out-group (like today's Roma people in Europe). Most of us will have had an experience of being in minority and out-group at the same time.

- Were you ever the only man among women, or the only woman among men?
- Only European among Africans, or only African among Europeans?
- Only blue-collar worker among white-collars, or only white-collar worker among blue-collars?
- Only sales person among financial staff, or only finance person among sales?

The list can go on forever. The good thing about these experiences is, I believe, that you can transfer this feeling and feel empathy for someone else in a minority or out-group - as long as you try. Storytelling increases our ability to feel empathy, remember?

We can also train ourselves to become more aware of our behaviours, whether we exclude others or include others by our actions. Having an open mind helps, as well as the ability to avoid jumping to conclusions right away. Easier said than done, because it's something we do all the time.

According to cognitive behaviour psychology, we tend to interpret what we see before we make an objective analysis of the situation. We interpret very quickly, based on previous experience and values. There are several tools one can use to become more aware of the internal process (for instance the relatively well known "Ladder of Inference" by Peter Senge). I often use a simple exercise from psychology called "D.I.E"; Description (see), Interpretation (think), Evaluation (feel). The question to ask oneself is: "Do I have enough data or description to really make a judgement?" Most of the time we benefit from getting more data and looking for more perspectives or interpretations of the person or the situation.

Inclusion is a broad term, and as mentioned before, not easy to translate. It encompasses many subjects, therefore this chapter is a mix of many aspects within diversity.

Continuing on the subject of busy lives from the chapter on *Gender and Freedom*, here is an article about the time squeeze we experience and how to create a more inclusive work environment.

Inclusive Behaviours and the Time Squeeze

(Published in *Diversity Journal* March 15, 2013) Having 'enough time' seems to be a luxury most people don't have these days. In Norway one can often read about *tidsklemma*, which is translated to "the time squeeze". This is often referred to as a challenge for parents with children and full-time jobs, but it is not limited to just this group. A modern person is drawn in many directions - work (and staying up-to-date, like attending courses, getting certifications/more degrees, etc.), children, household duties, aging parents, sports, networks, charity, friends, and hobbies.

There have been several 'waves' of downsizing and cutting costs in the workplace over the years, but it has tightened with the financial crisis.

People are laid off, but tasks aren't - rather the contrary - and with the expectation to be more efficient, since there is advanced technology available. I hear via my clients, friends, and networks that people are wondering when this will end; they are feeling exhausted by the pressure.

We have been aware of these issues for a while, but I'm questioning whether they have grown of late. Smartphones, videoconferences, and global travel - we are always on the move and expected to be available and responsive. I am noticing a certain fatigue on that front, evidenced by few replies, no thank yous (politeness is not a priority), and answering only one of two or three questions. This may be due to a large workload, but I would argue that it is too often at the cost of reduced concentration, mediocre results, and irritated people.

So what happens to the *inclusive environment* when people constantly feel squeezed for time?

It's not necessarily all negative. On a personal level it can feel good to accomplish many projects within a short timeframe and to work at a high speed - both give a feeling of achievement. But the challenge is that we can't be doing that all the time. Chances are we behave rather hostilely at work if there is too much pressure - and we are probably not very solutions-oriented. It is very likely that our focus narrows down, and that *inclusive behaviors* becomes an estranged theory. The fact is we need to slow down at times and have time to recharge our batteries. That's when we realize we haven't asked how our colleague has been for the last six months; that's when we take time to say thank you, or when we consider a problem from diverse angles. On whom does the responsibility lie for that? Well, certainly with ourselves, for example, by making sure to take time off. It also helps to ask ourselves questions like: How can I be more organized? What is important here? Where can I take control? What activities take energy and what activities give me energy? How can I balance them? Where are my limits?

And by that, I invite you to ask yourself certain questions. Are you sure that the deadline is crucial and non-negotiable? Are you certain you can't ask for help? Do you really think that you would lose your job if you propose delegating certain tasks?

All that said, it would be wrong to argue that responsibility lies entirely with the individual. An employer has systemic responsibility to set up a work structure that helps people get work done within a regular workday. Unreasonable pressure is a lose-lose for employee and employer and certainly doesn't foster a friendly work environment. It sure is more pleasant to work in a company where everyone feels of importance and that they are listened to. An inclusive work place produces happy, creative, innovative, loyal, productive employees - and as we know, that's good for the bottom line.

*

Stretching the content of this article a bit further, I sometimes wonder whether people are slaves of their own perceptions. For example, do you have to stay in a job you don't like - are you sure there aren't other options in life? What would life be like if you had less money, a slower pace, and more time?

When we talk about inclusion, *micro-inequities* are often mentioned. These are the things that are difficult to complain about, because each comment in itself is not very harmful, but it is the accumulation that might bring a person down, or even create a non-productive workplace. I wrote a blog about this in regards to some injustices I heard around me, the focus being on women.

The Power of Words

You may have heard of *micro-inequities*, or 'little things mean a lot'. In the workplace we talk about micro-inequities when an employee gets constant little comments that make she or he feel excluded or not accepted. It could also include actions like not being invited for a coffee or a lunch. The long-term effect can lead to depression or that the employee leaves the company.

As the person(s) who make the comments may not be conscious of the effect of his/her comments, it is recommended to inform this person that the comments are hurtful.

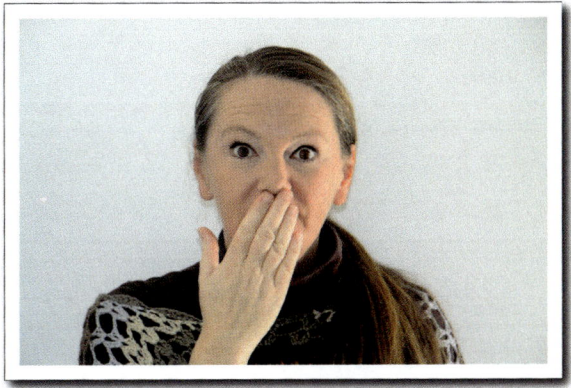

Outside work we also experience micro-inequities, and I would say that women experience it rather often. For example, when I first arrived in France, I learnt that;

o Women are not allowed to speak on behalf of the married couple when changing a telephone subscription.
o People often refer to the husband being the owner of all property.

And generally speaking women often hear comments about the 'truth' of women being bad drivers or not fit for a particular job. Singled out, these things don't seem much, and it is likely that there is *no bad intention*, but in totality it can give a subconscious feeling of being worth less. And we know that many women have a tendency to lack confidence.

About a year ago I read about a new *language culture* that has come into the high schools in Norway. The girls are increasingly called *whores* and *bitches* as a kind of slang, influenced by both immigration and movies. After a study in the schools where these words wore commonly used, it was found that the girls have decreased self-confidence and an increased focus on their appearance.

One could argue that the picture is more complex than blaming it on use of language only, but it clearly has an effect. Words are power, they can exclude and include.

Using a positive example regarding words and their impact, you might have seen the video *The Power of Words* on YouTube. In short; a lady passes by a blind man begging for money. Next to him there is a sign that says "I'm blind, please help". She stops and changes the words, which leads to the blind man getting more money. At the end of the work day the woman passes again and the blind man asks; "What did you write? She answered that she had changed the words to "It's a beautiful day and I can't see it". (The link to the advertisement is in the reference list.)

*

Seeing reality from someone else's perspective can be a challenge. As mentioned at the beginning of this chapter, some people say that one can transfer experiences and by that means obtain a sense of a similar situation. For instance being the only black person among whites, you can get the sense of being the only woman among men. Others say that it is not possible; you have to really have had the experience to understand. I tend to think that most of us are wise enough to be able to transfer experiences, or at least have empathy for situations that we have not lived. But, even if I think we *are* wise enough, sometimes we need others to point things out for us and explain, which is what triggered this blog.

<u>Walk in Someone Else's Shoes</u>

... That's what I proposed to a young, intelligent man I met in a training session. We were three people around a lunch table, having an interesting discussion about culture, particularly French culture. I mentioned that the pressure on women to always look slim, attractive and well-groomed is much higher than my own culture. And then, the surprise hit me. My lunch companion insisted that women, at least in his own culture (Serbian), want to always look their best, even when they go to the supermarket. I could not quite believe him, so I asked: "Do you always want to look good, 24 hours a day, 7 days a week?" "And do you appreciate getting comments every time you have a bad hair day, or are not dressed according to the taste of the other gender?". He didn't think it was the same thing, but we agreed on a challenge; that he would imagine himself as a woman in various situations when he was back home. Just to see whether he might experience another perspective.

It still surprises me when heterosexuals insist that homosexuals have no problems in today's society, or when men insist that women have the same opportunities as men in the workplace, or when the native population claims that the second generation immigrants have the same job opportunities as them. It should be enough to open a newspaper to see that it's not the case, but I suppose we all practise *selective reading and listening.*

Social equality and justice have gotten much better, compared to 60 years ago, say. Most countries these days have laws that protect, help and promote minority groups. But, I think we have a way to go before we create an equal society where differences are understood and appreciated. Staying within our comfort zone, staying within our own majority groups is so much easier. However, 'walking in someone else's shoes', to open your eyes, doesn't have to be so dramatic. You could for example;

- o Imagine you are in a wheelchair next time you take the underground, how would you go about it?
- o Ask someone at work from a different culture than your own how she or he experiences the work place and opportunities (you need to create a trusting environment for the person to open up).
- o Read statistics and insights about women and careers.
- o Discuss with someone gay, lesbian, bisexual or transgender about how they talk about their private lives at work.

*

Talking about staying within your 'comfort zone', a way to attain new perspectives and increase understanding of others and by that promote inclusion, is exactly to get out of that comfort zone. I went to a D&I training course for a week once, and one of the exercises we had to do was to pretend being gay and walk about the town to observe the reactions we got.

The reactions were very mixed, which was interesting in itself. This was in The Netherlands, a country that is considered liberal, at least concerning sexuality. In people's faces I saw anything from curiosity, to clear interest in joining the two of us, to irritation, and neutrality. I didn't mind the looks, whatever they were, but it felt tiring after a while to pretend to be someone I was not. I could only imagine how tiring it must be to pretend every day, all year... something many LGBT people do.

I don't think we will miraculously 'see the light' by exercises like the one I just described, but I do think we can increase our understanding by trying, and that this benefits the people around us, at work and in general.

Getting Out of Your Comfort Zone - What Does it Mean?

About 14 years ago I was advised to *get out of my comfort zone*, I think it was during my first official yearly performance feedback session in a large international company. At the time, I had no idea what that meant practically. I was hired to do a certain job and this 'out of comfort zone task' wasn't described to me... As I was new to the company and a lot of things (like unwritten rules) were unfamiliar, I didn't ask what I was expected to do.

Later on I experienced it to be quite a jargon in the company, *everybody* was told to get out of their comfort zone. And I do agree that it is good for development. So what does it mean, really? It could be:

- Shadow a colleague in a department you might find challenging to work with.
- Going on an expat assignment.
- Using different behaviour techniques with different people (for example use indirect language when your style is direct).
- Trying to be introvert when your natural preference is to be extravert.
- Using language of *feeling* when your inclination is to be rational and showing no emotion.
- Basically do something you do not usually do.

And what is the effect? You start to see other ways of how things can be solved and handled. You understand that there are more perspectives, more angles. You may start using the new behaviours you have practiced sometimes, when you see fit. Maybe you realize there is a middle way between two opposites, or that each end of the opposites has its own purpose. Possibly you have increased your repertoire so that you can comfortably move in a wider range of territory, like talking with people you have never talked with before. Which means that your comfort zone has increased.

On a wider scale, for example in business, having employees that are willing to increase their scope and see more perspectives, results in a more inclusive environment.

But how long should you stay in the 'uncomfortable zone'? Well, you can't be there all the time, you will exhaust yourself! If you are an emotional person, you can't stay cool and distant all the time, but you can dip in and out of it, to get the experience. Certain uncomfortable zones become comfortable over time, like a challenging project, but it may not be a good idea to *always* take on a challenging project (possible burnout).

Good luck with your journeys in the land of uncomfortable zones!

*

Life at work can be quite competitive, and it is not always easy to be heard. Being able to listen to others and to give them space, are good contributors to an inclusive work environment. Culture comes into play here, whether it is national, gender or corporate. Culture or not, listening is a skill we can all learn, and it has an immediately positive effect.

Do You See People?

I think I am on safe ground when I say that we all like to be listened to, to be given space or taken seriously, to have people laugh at our jokes, that people can see what we represent, that we feel *seen* as individuals. However, in the workplace and in our private lives this is actually quite a challenge. Very often we *don't* feel respected, seen or heard.

I have noticed that there are lots of books and training out there on communication or rather how to communicate better. There are a range of books in the Neuro-Linguistic Programming (NLP) school of thought, there are a zillion books with titles like *How to improve your communication skills*, and then you have related niche books like *The Art of Reading Thoughts*. Additionally, we have cross-cultural communication skills, which is one of my playing fields.

If you know a bit about different linguistic communication styles, you may have noticed that depending on people's linguistic culture they may overlap when you talk or they may pause to wait for you to speak. Funny things happen when people from a *wait culture* meet the *overlap culture*... The word *rude* comes to mind. Yet, they are not, they are just following their own linguistic style.

Then we have indirect communication versus direct communication, styles which may vary even within the same country. The direct person finds the indirect person difficult to understand (never being clear) and the indirect person feels the direct person is being blunt ("Can you turn it down, please?"). The communication style becomes a block; they cannot see each other (the intent) because the words get in the way.

Coming back to the books, I see a commonality through it all, which is to learn to observe, keep an open mind and try to meet people half-way. I find it fascinating that there is so much material on how to read people, and when you break it down to the core all we basically need to do is to;

o slow down,
o give space
o and LISTEN.

That will make people feel seen. Piece of cake.

On the subject of giving space, next is a further elaboration on that.

<u>Giving Space</u>

A family-in-law member had had an operation and I went to visit her in the hospital. After a while more visitors came. And then, to my surprise, one of the visitors 'claimed the space' and dominated the conversation with all her worries and own health problems. It continued throughout the time we spent there, getting various attention from various visitors. It really made me feel uneasy. We were there to talk with the person in hospital. She was, or should have been, the person in focus.

Recognize it? The person who dominates in classes, constantly wanting to answer to show how good/clever/smart she or he is. Not allowing time and space for others to contribute. Or the person in work meetings who keeps hammering her or his idea, without giving the chance for others to share theirs. You just feel like kicking them in a certain place, don't you?

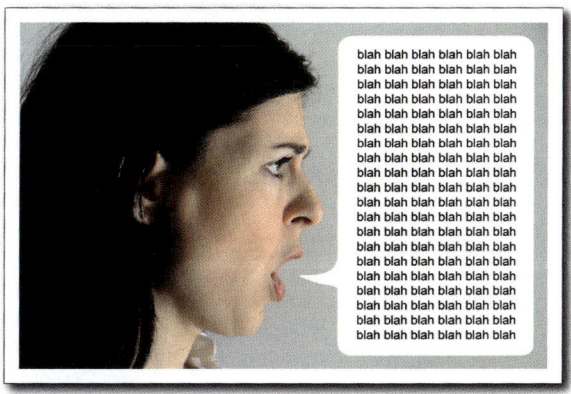

So what's that about? I can only guess, and of course there are individual differences, but I can think of a few reasons;

- Cultural differences; e.g. the French are taught to convince others of their ideas. Weakness is that they want to convince so much that they forget to listen.
- Strong desire to present their idea as the best, or a strong desire to participate in a learning experience. Weakness is that there is no space to hear other ideas and learnings.
- Strong need to be noticed. This is walking into a psychological field that I don't have the competency to talk intelligently about, but my impression is that some people have not been notice in the earlier part

of their life and need to compensate. It creates a stressful environment for the person and the people around them.
- o Lack of awareness ; i.e. someone who has grown up in a large family needs to develop the ability to be heard. In a business setting this may be an advantage, but not always. Key is understanding when to use the skill and when to put it on hold.

What can a manager, colleague, class mate, facilitator, friend, *do*? I'd have to say "Not easy. You don't want to cool down someone's enthusiasm and energy that's positive for all. A facilitator or a manager probably has the easiest job here, by saying things like "That's great/ love the idea/ thanks for the input, but I also would like to hear from others to build on that and widen the scope". People on the same level, colleagues, class mates, friends, have a bit more of a tricky job, but they can also use the same strategy with some charm; "Great/ love it/ oh that's interesting, *and* let's hear what others think about it and share their thoughts."

Being able to give space to others, or even letting others shine, requires some maturity and also confidence in oneself. But, sometimes it's just a blind spot that needs to be pointed out in a helpful and polite manner.

...which leads me to talk about teams and inclusion... "Researchers found that properly managed and trained diverse work teams produced results that were six times higher than homogenous teams." - Dr. Edward Hubbard, *The Business Case for Diversity*

High-Performing Teams or Happy Teams?

The term *high-performing teams* is almost worn out in the world of business and team-building in particular. Everybody wants high-performing teams. But what does it mean? I think it means *happy teams*, because people who enjoy their jobs and feel good about the way they are treated at work produce more and give more of themselves to the people around them.

So how do you get happy teams and make sure their strengths are utilized (both as individuals and as a group)? There are, as I am sure you know, a few hundred theories about it and consulting companies earn lots of money finding solutions to that question.

Personally, I think the key is a simple word; the word is *inclusion*. Rather than giving you a well-documented recipe on how to build happy teams, I would like to share some personal experiences and invite you to reflect on my findings.

I have more than twenty years' work experience, and I have been working in two high-performing/happy teams. What did these two teams have in common?

- o Tangibles: A clear, outspoken and repeated vision and mission. Clear job description. Regular team meetings. Structured performance management.
- o Non-tangibles: A strong wish among the team-members to succeed. Humour. Acceptance of emotions. Respect. Support. Focus on strengths and using these strengths. Acceptance of differences. Feeling proud of colleagues and being part of the team.

In one of the teams the connectivity was strengthened by using communication tools like chatting on Instant Messenger, structured telephone team meetings, spontaneous individual telephone calls and regular email contact. Even though a virtual team, it didn't feel like it. In the other team, there was a culture for sharing mistakes, as it was considered to heighten learning for everyone. In this team humour was an important factor of the team spirit which led to increased energy and productivity (moneywise it was the highest performing team in the company).

As you can see from the above, the non-tangible list is longer than the tangible one. What does it tell you? What would you add to the two lists when you think of your own experiences of working in successful teams?

*

Including people's personal background in teams is sometimes an advantage, depending on the project and the nature of the team, but it can also lead to dilemmas. I have one example from when I ran interviews on *How inclusive is our work environment?* for a French branch of an international company. In one of the groups an employee of North-African descent shared that she was never asked about the know-how of her culture, although it was relevant to her work. She thought it was because of French law, that one is not allowed to register employees' ethnicity. She felt this dilemma was a lost opportunity for her employer, and that her ethnicity did at times feel like a taboo subject. It was mentioned in several groups I interviewed that diversity was underplayed in the company, the aim being to find similarities across cultures, not differences. One could ask why didn't the North-African lady bring it up herself ? Hierarchy comes into play and respecting the decision of the manager not to talk about it.

From teams to language - which I mentioned in the chapter about culture. But language is more than 'just culture', it is also a tool that one can use to include and exclude others.

Language as an Inclusional Tool

Many years ago I attended an international school. In the school, as in real life, people from the same nationalities tended to stay together. Attracted to the safety that it represents to be with people who speak the same language and understand the same customs and codes in unfamiliar settings. All the minority foreigners (as we were all foreigners), had to mingle with the other large groups. And what happened? A lot of the time they could not participate in the conversations, because the majority group spoke their mother tongue, rather than the joint language: English. After a while a new group emerged, one with a mix of minority foreigners. I think they gained a lot more out of their stay abroad than those who stayed with their fellow countrymen and -women.

Language is power, they say. I suppose it was originally meant for people within the same country, splitting between those who could read, write and master the language elegantly and those who couldn't. Today the scope is bigger. In large international companies the ones who speak fluently the main company language is at an advantage over others. And they can use the language as a tool: to include and to exclude. People in general prefer to feel part of a group, to belong. Choosing to speak a language that not everyone understands, is a very strong exclusional technique that has efficient results if the aim is to make someone feel like an outsider. But, most of the time, we are probably just not aware of our own impact in groups with different language skills.

So, what are good language inclusion behaviours?

- When in a group, speak a language that everyone understands. I know it is easier to slip into the mother tongue or a language you master well, but the group will benefit from the input of a person with a different background.
- Let people try to express themselves, even if it takes them longer than you. The dance around the subject might actually bring something to the conversation. If they ask for help on translation, that's the moment to offer the word they are looking for.
- Ask your colleague if she or he wants to be corrected in grammar, offering it as a gift to improve.
- Be open for 'creative' styles of expressing a situation (it's great when people think of a saying in their own language and try to do an instant and direct translation - wonderful new perspectives!)
- If your language level is much higher than those in your group, try to use more common words and avoid regional jargon.

When talking about inclusion at work or in social settings, I often think about micro-inequities, or 'little things mean a lot'. I think it is worth repeating that the little things we say and do, when added up, can have a strong positive or negative effect on others. Being aware of our impact makes the difference.

*

If you have attended a team-building event, or maybe training on diversity and inclusion, you will probably have come across the *iceberg*. It is often used as an illustration of people; what we see - above the water line - and what we don't see - below the water line. As you know, the iceberg has a bigger mass below water. At work we seldom have the time to get to know our colleagues and understand what is below the waterline of their iceberg. It might not even seem appropriate, depending on our cultural backgrounds. However, as the following blog will illustrate, at times it is very useful to dig a little bit deeper and get to know people more than just superficially.

Seeing Beyond

How often do you ask your colleague what s/he does in her/his out-out-work hours? How often do you ask about their development interests?

Some people naturally ask and stay curious about the lives of colleagues, friends and acquaintances. And some companies cater for this curiosity in team-building events and regular team meetings. But, I must admit, looking back at my work experience, the information I get through my coaching clients, and the feedback I get personally from my general environment, I have the impression that the majority of people don't have time or are not used to thinking and seeing beyond the first impression they get of a person.

Having a limited view of a person's competencies, strengths and interests may hinder good talent management. I remember an example of the opposite about eight years ago when a manager I know took a 'risk' and brought a secretary into a communications role. It was based on her interests and the fact that she did a good job. This manager took the time to talk with the employee and think out of the box and the label *secretary* when she voiced the wish to move on. I remember the look on the manager's face when he shared with the rest of the team; "It's like seeing a flower going into full bloom!" Because he had the capacity to look beyond and look at the whole person, he got a very talented communications advisor.

As a coach I have heard several clients say that the feedback they get is either a limited part of who they are or it may be plain wrong because people only see the mask and not the person behind it. This can be quite frustrating; it feels like being put in a box isn't yours. People see a snapshot of who you are and then come to the conclusion that "this is it". I see some cases where this is a strong barrier to development, because an individual has been told so many times that he is 'cold' and therefore not suited for a job where he helps people. Actually, the person is just shy, and his warmth comes out in one-to-one relations.

Another example is meeting people who do not speak your language fluently. Your impression may be; "He doesn't speak much", "She is impolite", "She has no opinions" or "Gosh, he uses a lot of words to get to the point". All of this may be due to lack of language skills. Ask them to say a few words in their mother tongue and you will see more of their personality!

Having the capacity to see beyond is helpful when you are a manager, a recruiter, an HR professional or any kind of advisor. Actually, when I think of it, it is useful to anyone, at any time. When you show interest in someone else, you may notice that they light up, that they are happy that someone cares enough to ask about their opinion or their input or experience or wishes. They feel included. Being curious about someone may change the energy in that relationship; you may find that your colleague, boss, employee, mother/father-in-law, brother/sister, etc., etc. become easier to collaborate with if you show them some interest. Everyone can work up the curiosity-muscle; stay curious about people - just ask, ask, ask!

*

Being *inclusive* is also coloured by our cultural background. Who do we include ? Everybody or just those who matter? Who matters ? It might depend on your relationship with hierarchy, and as we know that varies a lot around the world. The next blog is clearly coloured by my own egalitarian set of values. Someone from a hierarchical culture might still see the use of these examples. Creating a large *in-group* in a company will likely get the best out of its employees.

Inclusive Behaviours and Seeing Things in a Wider Context

As mentioned some pages ago, in my early twenties I got in touch with a culture that was very different to mine; I moved to Cyprus. I experienced that there were different rules and social contexts. One thing that I really liked, was the exchange of recommendations and services; an attitude of "I'm nice to you, you'll be nice to me". I worked as a PR Manager in a hotel, which seemed to materially influence many service people around town so that they were very nice to me!

Although this *special treatment* made me smile and sometimes made me feel a bit awkward, I found the general attitude pleasant, and good for business. I think it helps to enlarge your perspectives, seeing that so many of us are connected and we have an influence on each other. If you think of an office environment, having a good rapport with people at any level of the organisation, turns out to be beneficial at times you don't expect it to. For example you get time on someone's busy agenda because you know her or his secretary, or you ease smoothly into a new team because you have chatted with these people in the company restaurant, or you get good recommendations from colleagues for a new job/promotion (because you treat them with respect instead of seeing them as competitors), or you have a good relationship with your new boss as she or he was a good colleague of yours before. People move around: you never know, the janitor (that someone wasn't nice to) may be a management student working during his/her studies and all of a sudden she or he is that someone's boss.

It amazes me that people don't think of the above examples as a possibility. When I hear of, or meet, people who don't reply, or reply impolitely, because you are not 'important' in their eyes, there might be a picture and a context they are failing to see. It might actually backfire one day. So, can you help these people to 'open their eyes'? It goes back to values, doesn't it, what values are important? Is it egalitarianism - to treat everyone with the same respect and importance? Or is rather that respect and attention are given to people of a certain position or status? If you are a colleague or the boss of someone who only prioritizes work coming from high up in the hierarchy, you could try to find personal motivating factors for this person to see the importance of being nice to *everybody*. That person may also have another value that can be triggered. Or maybe it isn't just this person? Then it would be an idea to look at it systemically; is this a general attitude or culture within the office, do we need to implement peer reviews as part of the performance cycle or do we need to consider an action plan to increase inclusiveness among us?

Changing behaviours isn't easy, but it's possible. It sure is more pleasant to work in an environment where everyone feels important, that they are listened to, heard, and seen - and get a response! And… research shows that an inclusive work place produces happy, creative, innovative, loyal, productive employees - and as we know, that has an impact on the company's performance.

*

Going slightly 'off-piste', as it were, I would like to elaborate on the word I used in the last paragraph: *creativity*. A skill that is important these days and which creates a feeling of mastery, using all of you and having fun at work.

Inspiration, Creativity, Mindfulness

I remember seeing a video of a speech that John Cleese made about creativity. He said the *most creative people* are those who see the value in doing nothing, having fun, just for the sake of it, with no purpose.

Let me say that again: "doing nothing, having fun, no purpose". Sounds mind-blowing to most people in corporate jobs, and generally in our western society focused on *doing, results,* and *action.*

It makes sense however, when we bring *mindfulness* into the picture. To calm down to be able to speed up. To stop so that we can see the beauty around us. To seek stillness so we can manage the noise.

A client told me that she was so glad when her computer broke down one day (it was just for a day). That would be a nightmare for most people. But guess what, she was forced to do something else with her time, for example painting the house - and that's when inspiration came! Not trying to force it through in front of the computer.

How often do we think about getting some fresh air before an important meeting? Maybe that would help negotiation, finding solutions, bringing out ideas? When would we ever think about going to the beach for an hour before finishing a report? Maybe it would give us more energy and the possibility to write *in flow*? Most of us would rather dip our nose deeper into the office air and work as a mouse in a wheel. Because that's what we do!

There are companies that are dependent on their worker's creativity and therefore provide more space for flexible schedules and different ways of working. But, I think us 'regular' people can also break more often out of the standard and create our own creative space. Even if it is just a simple thing like a three-minute guided meditation (there are several books and CD's available to aid with this) can help you recharge in a busy day.

Try something different one day, be bold! And enjoy more inspiration, creativity and mindfulness.

*

From the general to the more specific, the next few blogs are about two areas of diversity: LGBT (Lesbian, Gay, Bi-sexual and Transgender) and people with disabilities. For clarity, you might come across the abbreviation LGBT as well as GLBT (Gay, Lesbian).

Starting with LGBT, it made me think of a discussion we had in a training session I gave in Norway back in 2012. "This isn't a problem in Norway" was the comment from a participant when I mentioned that Witeck-Combs/Harris Interactive found that "78% of Gay, Lesbian,

Bisexual, Transgender (GLBT) and their friends/relatives would switch brands to companies that are known to be GLBT-friendly". It is true that Norwegian society is fairly open, however reports tell us that people still experience stereotyping, discrimination and prejudice. The majority tends to see things from the majority perspective and this discussion reminded me of that. A Norwegian or not, fact is that if one travels as a gay person to countries like Iran, Mauritania, Saudi Arabia, Sudan and Yemen, as well as parts of Nigeria and Somalia, one could risk the death penalty by being out in the open. And one would not be safe in India either, as they have re-instated a law against homosexuality as of 2013.

An LGBT Inclusive Work Environment

Some times I forget how much feelings and reactions there are around the subject being Lesbian, Gay, Bi-sexual or Transgender. I have been in a work and private environment for quite some time where this isn't an issue, and therefore I don't think about it being such a sensitive subject until someone makes a remark. But one day someone *did* make a remark that I did not approve of.

I was invited to a lunch where someone was telling a story about a co-worker she didn't work well with. She said; "I get along with everyone, but this one I really struggle to co-operate with". She then found the 'explanation', according to herself. Her boss had informed her that the colleague is lesbian. "That explains it", she told us. "Explains what?", I said. "Well, that's why she is acting so strange", was the response. I then commented that it is probably her colleague's character that she reacts to, not the fact that she is gay. Another guest agreed with me, but this particular person was completely convinced that the reason for her colleague's odd behaviour was due to her being lesbian. To help her see another perspective, I would have loved to elaborate more on the subject or even show her the video *Growing up Gay* by Brian McNaught, but I am not really sure how receptive she would have been.

As individuals, we choose how much we want to inform ourselves on various subjects and how open we want to be to others who are not like us. A company however, has a certain ethical obligation to inform and create an inclusive environment for their employees.

*

In many workplaces being gay is mostly a non-subject, it is not talked about. Surveys show however, that many employees spend a lot of energy hiding the gender of the person they live with. A simple exercise you could try yourself, is to spend a week saying *he* instead of *she* or *vice-versa* when you talk about your partner. You will likely find out that it takes some of your brain capacity, a capacity you could have used more constructively.

I have learned from colleagues that it is very tiring to *come out* all the time, which is what it feels like every time you mention anything about your personal life to a new colleague or in a new work environment. However, in a workplace where inclusion is at the forefront, this is not an issue - people are who they are and speak freely about it. In my 25 years of work experience, I have worked in two departments like that.

On a more personal note, I have friends and several family and in-law family members who are transgender, lesbian or bi-sexual. I remember a family member who is transgender telling me what a relief it was when she met her now-wife. She said, "For the first time, I can be just me". It's something that is also between the lines of the story from Thaïs that you can read in a couple of paragraphs. Yet, I admit that I have never had a deep conversation with my Norwegian family members regarding; "In what way has being in a minority been a problem for you?" I have asked myself why and the answer is: lack of private moments to ask such a question. I should find out whether such a question would be appreciated and create that private moment with my family in Norway.

The degree of how difficult it is to be open about being lesbian, gay, bi-sexual or transgender depends on many factors, including culture and generations. The young student Thaïs in France shares her experiences on her surroundings' reactions to her having a girlfriend.

"I was not gay before I met the person who is now my girlfriend. Now I consider myself both heterosexual and homosexual, in other words, I'm 'bi'. I prefer to say that I fell in love with a person rather than falling in love with a girl. I met her on the internet. Not on a dating site, but totally by chance on YouTube. We exchanged comments and emails, and then we met in person. She declared herself first. I was sixteen then, and I had never considered our relationship as anything else than a friendly one. I made her wait for several weeks, and then I decided to allow myself this forbidden love. Because I love her, that's all. That we are both girls is complicating the situation, but it does not change my feelings.

"My parents took it badly. In addition to being a girl, my girlfriend is four years older than me, so that's a double disadvantage. My mother warned me; assuring me that it was not love I felt for her, but a sisterly feeling that I misunderstood for love. My father laughed. He joked constantly with a lot of offensive remarks and stereotypes about lesbians. I do not think he realized how much he was hurting me. They no longer wanted to see my girlfriend. They both hoped it was a phase and that growing up, I would eventually find a nice and cute boy. Now that I'm nineteen years old and our relationship has lasted nearly three years, things are better between her and my parents. She was able to return to our home very recently for the first time in three years. I think the passing of time helped.

"I still consider myself lucky. The boyfriend of one of my friends has almost been hunted by his parents because he was gay. My parents just needed time to accept.

"In high school things were easy. All my friends were very open, and some of them have even turned out to be homosexual or bisexual themselves. None of the people my age or a little older have ever made a comment. I must say that I do not shout it from the rooftops either. I check people's standing before I say that I have a girlfriend, for example I make sure to address the issue of homosexuality to understand the opinion of the person I am talking with. I only had one bad experience with someone of my age. It was one summer I was working during the holidays, one of my colleagues gave me a rather negative view of homosexuals. I remember very well that she said: "I could not be friends with a lesbian, I'd be too afraid ...". "Afraid of what?" I asked. "I do not know, it would be disturbing." And yet, we were friends. I decided not to tell her about my girlfriend, and lied to her, saying that the person I called every night was my boyfriend. I do not know how she learned the truth later, but her attitude changed completely. She became distant, and even started telling lies about me so that I would take distance to her and the others in the team.

"This "friend" was a Muslim, but I have had worse reactions from my grandparents who are very Catholic. I cannot tell them who I am. I really fear that the shock would be too severe, that it would hurt them. When the marriage law for gay people was passed in France, they were very outspoken against homosexuals, to such a level that they surprised me. I knew they were committed to the practise of good old heterosexual marriage in its traditional form, but I did not think they would be so hateful towards homosexuals, mainly to men. "Disgusting", "They are sick, they need to heal", "I do not believe that they can be shown on TV, it's hard to believe! What is happening to this world?" After these words, I could not admit that their "friend", whom they liked a lot and they often asked about, was actually my girlfriend. I am not planning to tell them. Imagine the thought that their perfect little girl, so talented at school, destined for a great future, would be a lesbian? Their world would collapse. I prefer to spare them this unnecessary stress.

"In conclusion, for me it is easier to talk to young people about this topic than adults. I think the world today is in movement and that more and more people are open-minded enough to accept such things. But I'm still shocked and find it incomprehensible that so many people participated in demonstrations in France against gay marriage. I do not feel particularly concerned, though, because I do not consider myself as exclusively homosexual, but as bisexual. However, I do not understand that one can be so seriously opposed to the happiness of someone else."

*

What I notice with Thaïs' story, is the fact that she switches between being herself and hiding parts of herself, depending on who she's with. She says that she checks what people think about homosexuality before she mentions her love life, and that she even lies about it not to offend people. Seems like walking a thin ridge at the top of a mountain, always watching your step.

Now moving onto people with disabilities. Or maybe we could rename this large group of people to *People with other Abilities*? Isn't it so that if you are blind, your hearing gets better?

The two first blogs cover various ways that might not easily be seen; it could be mental health or a physical challenge.

Hidden Disability

Recently a Norwegian politician *came out* as bipolar. She was interviewed on TV, sharing the challenges she has in her daily life, as well as what she feels she is gaining from being bipolar. She mentioned that her ups and downs make her appreciate the *ups* so much more, something other people possibly forget.

Our mental health is still something we do not share widely with people, although I would say it is less of a taboo than before. Well known people, like singer Robbie Williams and actor Ben Stiller, have publically informed that they are bipolar - which I do believe have contributed to more openness and acceptance of what one could call 'hidden disability/condition/impairment'.

I know that in France companies struggle to fulfill the government legislation of reserving 6% of the jobs for people with disabilities. It is assumed that quite a few employees have mental disabilities: they just do not inform their employer (see figure with data drawn from OECD, showing you are less likely to be employed if you have a mental disability).

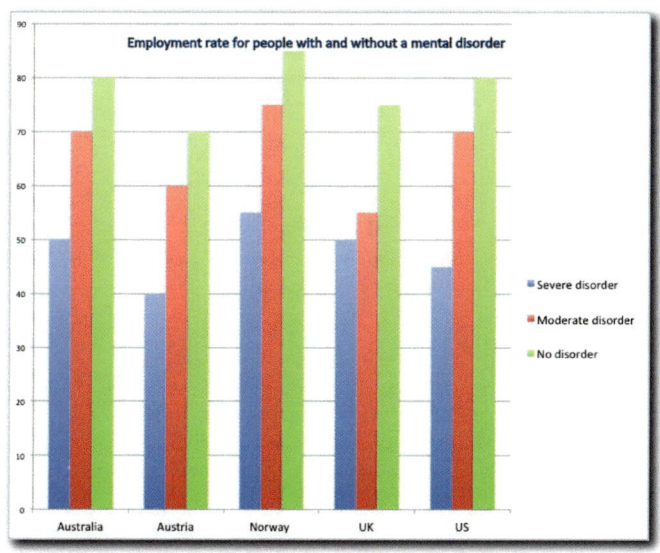

Mental health is still taboo enough that employees do not feel safe to 'come out' as someone with a mental illness. I read that some people feel safer coming out as gay or lesbian, than saying they have a mental illness. It is the fear of being stigmatized, the fear of not getting the projects and promotions that they believe they can rightfully earn. So what can be done? Awareness and education are the key words here.

And when I say awareness and education, I mean for *all* kinds of disabilities, whatever degree, whether visible or not. Over the years I have acquired knowledge from disability networks as well as published research that the main barrier to people with disabilities being hired and promoted is a lack of awareness among hiring managers. An awareness session with some facts and tips, let's say of a couple of hours' length, gives a good impact and start for behavioural change in a business. I have seen it happen. I was lucky to work for a company where many colleagues in D&I and HR felt passionately about hiring more people with disabilities. They conducted awareness sessions and followed up with managers and colleagues, hired more people with disabilities or impairments and clearly felt the environment and the company gained from it.

Coming back to hidden disabilities, what do you do and what does your company do to create an inclusive environment for staff to be open about their mental health?

« It Would Have Been Better if my Arm Had Been Cut off...

... then people would understand that I can't do the things that I used to do. »

This is a comment from someone close to me. And I think many with a hidden disability would recognize and empathize with this statement. In this particular case we are talking about tinnitus, or a constant noise in the ear. Can you imagine never hearing yourself talk, or being afraid that you shout, having trouble focusing or not sleeping - constantly feeling tired? It cannot be seen, but it makes a big impact on your life!

About fifteen years ago I had a hidden disability myself. I was fortunate in that it lasted only two years, something I am extremely thankful for. I had an inflammation in my right shoulder that after a while resulted in the whole shoulder and arm becoming 'dead'; I couldn't use it and I had pain 24 hours a day. But my disability couldn't easily be seen and people couldn't see my pain either. In a way it was good, because I didn't want to be labeled as 'someone with a problem', but on the other hand it was difficult, because I constantly had to explain why I couldn't do this or that. Funnily enough, this is what people remember of me when I meet someone from that period of my life. People tend to remember the negative things (which is actively used in the media) and I was indeed coupled with my disability label.

So, what can people without disabilities do to help and support the colleague, friend, family member with his or her disability? Observe. Ask. Respect.

- o Observe; is this a person who would like help? Or maybe who would get offended if offered help?
- o Ask; "How are you doing", or "Maybe you don't want me to ask?" "What can I do for you", or "What don't you want me to do?"
- o Respect; whatever the person tells you. Each person has her or his own way of dealing with the hidden disability. Some people prefer to keep it hidden, others prefer to have it out in the open. Also have enough respect for the person that you challenge her or him like you would do anyone else.

*

One person who doesn't mind talking about his hidden disability, is entrepreneur Kurt Lerbo, who lives in Norway.

"It's hard to say when I got ADHD (Attention Deficit Hyperactivity Disorder), but I suppose it must have been before the age of ten. The main challenge since then has been to concentrate on a task for a longer period of time. I have too many thoughts in my head simultaneously. People can't see this, of course, and at times I might be misunderstood.

"When I was I child I used to beat up the big boys in school as a strategy to stay safe. Since I moved schools seven out of nine school years, the teachers didn't really get to know me and they didn't understand the reason for my poor performance at school. When I was 15 I met a teacher who believed in me and encouraged me, and that's when I realized I could influence my concentration level to a certain degree, and my grades at school improved.

"Although I have always worked, and I am a reliable worker with exceptional capacity, life has been tough. Twenty years ago, at the age of 32

I was at a turning point; I was finally sober after the third stay in a detox clinic. Behind me I had a lifetime as an alcoholic and drug addict, I started drinking when I was ten. The doctors and psychologists at the clinic recommended that I go back to school; my dream was to become a nurse. I went happily to the unemployment office, which was the place where one could apply for a government supported education programme. The person in charge of the financial support, however, was not as enthusiastic as the doctors and psychologists at the clinic. He told me; "They can't decide whether you get financial support, and I don't believe in you. You don't have the resources to complete an education, you have used drugs for too long". I asked him how he could be so certain, and he accepted the challenge. He sent me on to a psychologist that he knew, who decided to give me three different intelligence tests - it took a whole day. The result showed that I probably have a minor brain injury, as a result of sniffing glue from the ages of 10 to 14. However, the psychologist came to the conclusion that with my life story, I had proved that when I really wanted something, I made it happen. I had also managed to perform well in jobs since the age of 16, despite my troubled relationship with alcohol and drugs. So, she supported my application.

"I then acquired the high school diploma in one year with top grades, which was followed by three years in nursing school, an education at university level. I also had to work in between studies to help my wife support our family of four children.

"In hindsight I realize that it was a great accomplishment, but nothing beats the achievement of staying sober, year after year."

*

Coming back to the image of an iceberg, we only see the tip of it. In Kurt's case, for many years people saw his hyper-activity, but not his potential. Luckily, he met some people who saw beyond that and gave him a chance, as a teenager and as an adult. His story also makes me think of the amount of people who use drugs to appear 'normal' at work.

There are more people with a hidden disability than you might think. According to Australian statistics (Australian Network on Disability), almost 90% of all disability is not visible. This includes conditions like sleeping disorders, diabetes, dyslexia, chronic pain or chronic fatigue and various forms of mental illnesses. It is very likely that you know someone with a hidden disability.

Some time ago I worked on a project to promote hiring people with disabilities in the key countries where my company was located. One of the major blocks was costs; "We don't have this in the budget", or "We need to adjust our building to a wheelchair user and it is too expensive". In some cases they were not aware that they were entitled to some funding from the state. And when implemented, surprise, surprise, some of the changes also benefited other staff, e.g those with non-spoken back/knee problems. And that's what I saw in several countries, there were surprising benefits, not only physical, but also a general impact on staff - for example seeing another perspective, a different way of handling practical challenges or a new approach to work. I remember a couple of countries conducted interviews with the teams where they had hired people with disabilities, mental or physical. In all cases but one, the teams were positive and felt they had gained something rather than added a burden to the workload. The latter was indeed a worry, that they would need to help their new colleague. They did have to help their colleague at the beginning, as one would with any newcomer.

Having had focus on people with disabilities for a while, I tend to picture myself in their shoes and consider their challenges, hence the two following blogs on physical disability.

Underground or Not to Underground?

When on business travel I often use the Paris Métro and London Underground. And each time I go down there I am surprised at how little accommodation there is for people with disabilities - and luggage-loaded travelers. Yes, there are some stops that cater for wheelchair users, but the majority of trains and entrances and exits are not accessible. I had a look at a guideline for wheel-chair users in London, and basically it tells you to contact staff for help. I wonder how many people feel that easy to do..

There is a site for Paris' tourists that covers the subject "is Paris accessible for people with disabilities?" And the answer is: "First, the bad news: Paris doesn't exactly have a stellar record where accessibility is concerned. Wheelchair-intolerant cobblestone streets; out-of-order or nonexistent Métro elevators; café bathrooms in basements accessible only by narrow spiral staircases- you name it. For visitors with disabilities or limited mobility, Paris can seem like an obstacle course." There is some good news, however: the RER train (overground) does have accessibility for wheelchair users in almost all stations.

One could say "Take a taxi!" It isn't the best option, I'd say. Paris and London are cities that are overcrowded with cars, taking a taxi may take you longer than using the underground and it is substantially more expensive. Not very fair to a group that may have less income due to their disability (generally speaking many struggle with getting employment). There are buses, of course, but they get stuck in traffic too - and in Paris I know that they don't have the same stops as the underground.

I am sure that building more lifts in the Underground/Métro would mean gigantic costs for any given city. But with an aging population I believe the need will only increase. When I think of it, there is a large group of people already who need lifts and escalators; people with a lot of luggage or groceries, people with small children, people who have knee or back pains, people with heart conditions, people who don't see well or not at all. Should be good enough reasons to work on finding the funding for improved public transport! Which hopefully would lead to less cars and better air...

Inclusion for People with Hearing Impairment

When moving to another country you naturally notice the things that are different to where you came from, whether it was your home country or another one. Something that I wondered about when moving to France, and I am still wondering about, is the fact that very few TV programmes have subtitles. Even many DVD's are not subtitled. Not very practical for people with hearing impairments, people who are deaf - and foreigners like me.

Diving into some facts and figures I have found out that approx 5 million of the French population are deaf or have a hearing impairment (2010 numbers according to Unapeda, an organisation for parents. Another site claims there are 6 million people with a hearing deficit, but there is no source). In 2005, the '*loi sur le handicap*' stated that all main French TV channels should subtitle 100% of their programmes from February 2010 - they had 5 years to implement the law. From what I can see; they have not taken action on it.

Whether there are 5 or 6 million people with a full or partial hearing impairment, the numbers are impressive (it is more than the whole population of Norway!!). So, why did this law come into place this late and why isn't it being put into practice as it should? The people I have asked don't know, but I have read that the TV channels got complaints from viewers that the subtitles disturbed them. I know people who say the same if we put a video with subtitles. My conclusion is that it is a matter of habit, the French population has grown up with dubbed TV and reading subtitles is like all of a sudden having to start to write with the left hand being right-handed. For the TV channels it is probably a question of costs as well.

This makes me think of a dilemma; why should the majority change their habits for the minority? In another situation, I would probably encourage a comprehensive debate around such a question, but in this case... Frankly speaking, I don't think this is a very difficult habit to change for the majority, and it makes a huge difference for the minority. *That's* inclusion.

*

As mentioned above, the business world might only see the obstacles by hiring people with disabilities - until they have actual experience of doing

so. Unfortunately, many people who would like to and are able to work, don't get that chance. The consequence is that businesses are missing out on talent and quite a few countries are paying welfare to people who could actually pay for themselves. Loss-loss situation.
Next is a blog on the opposite situation. This is a success story that I hope will inspire the reader.

Seeing Opportunities Where Other's Don't

In 2013 I read an article about an IT company called Unicus in Norway that has hired several employees with Asperger's Syndrome. It is a profitable business with an employee pool of unique talents (the managing director mentioned one employee that learned Japanese on his own, another can read 2000 words per minute). These are talents that most companies wouldn't even bring in for an interview. Unicus has calculated that they save the Norwegian government 1,375, 000 euros for just ONE of their employees, as they are now working and not on welfare.

About two years ago I saw a TV programme in France about a factory that hired only people with disabilities, which is also a profitable business. I'm sure there are more companies like this around Europe, but it isn't common.

Feedback from the employees in both examples above is that they are very happy to be able to contribute to society and not feel like a burden. They earn money, they socialize and feel valued. Quite the opposite of the feelings of staying home, on welfare. Feedback from the employers is that they get extremely loyal employees that never miss a day of work. And special talents, as mentioned in the first paragraph. I have read and heard about same kind of feedback in *regular* companies that have a small staffing percentage of people with disabilities. Win-win.

Some years back I worked in a company that had a person born blind answering incoming calls. No one could hear that she was blind, as she had all the equipment she needed to transfer calls and read absent messages. She was the best first impression of the company you can imagine: friendly and helpful - and always there. Those people are not easy to find. The investment cost of getting the equipment she needed is not even a percent of the cost saved in hiring and re-hiring for 30 years. People with sight impairments is a group that very often get isolated, which wasn't the case for her. The job allowed her the money to have more freedom to do what she wanted, and a social life. Win-win.

So, why is it so hard for employers to see the win-win by hiring people with physical and mental disabilities? Lack of information? Lack of will? Fear of additional work? Fear of having 'awkward situations' arising at work? I believe it is the first; lack of information. Many businesses don't know the investment costs (how much and what is covered by the government), they don't know how to advertise jobs externally that doesn't put off people with disabilities, and they are not aware of the benefits of hiring people with disabilities.

What can create more win-win situations? Off the top of my head, I'd say three core actions; invite a specialist to enlighten the management team(s), look at recruitment strategies and processes, focus on creating an inclusive work environment.

What do you think ?

Final remarks

There can be no diversity without inclusion. I remember an HR Manager I talked with in The Netherlands who struggled to meet a diversity target in a factory. She said: "I can put someone from Morocco there tomorrow, but unless I work on preparing the work environment first, he will leave the following day".

This chapter on Inclusion has covered a lot of terrain. What is a simple way of looking at it? What can one choose to do as of tomorrow to *become inclusive*, or to work towards a more inclusive work environment? Here are some basic ideas :

- Do I share talking space? How much do I speak and how much do I listen?
- Do I show respect of others' opinions?
- How is my body language, and do I keep eye contact with everyone when in a group setting?
- What do I do if someone uses demeaning language in front of someone I know or tells a stereotyped joke?
- Do I ask all of my colleagues to go for lunch? Do I invite my colleagues in another country for a *virtual coffee chat*?
- As a manager; do I listen to all, do I share information with all, do I encourage ideas, do I invite people to talk?
- In my team and in team meetings; do we *talk about how to talk*?

What else? What would you include?

CHAPTER EIGHT:
THAT'S ALL, FOLKS

You have read a number of stories and considered a few perspectives in this book. But, they are far from all-encompassing of the challenges, angles, possibilities and solutions within the topics I have covered. I have shared some of my experiences and thoughts, as well as those of some guest writers. There is so much more out there, many more angles to be considered and so much more to learn. As my mother used to say: "It's fun to live and see how it goes!"

Life is a discovery !

As you might have read between the lines, I am an idealist, I wish for a fair world. However, I do know that an ideal world does not exist; we humans try and fail - and succeed. We do have more equality than five decades ago, and the younger generations are generally more exposed to and seem more accepting of other cultures and other ways of seeing life.

Regarding diversity and inclusion work, I also think every drop of progress counts. I am happy when I see an African or Middle Eastern person on French TV, when I see participants in the song contest *The Voice* who are blind or with a speaking impairment, when I see another successful woman as a top politician or at managerial level. It means that fighting for something works, that we are in movement and that what was considered impossible 50 years ago, is a reality today. The next 50 years - it's up to us to make the world we want to live in.

CHAPTER NINE:
FOR STUDENTS AND DISCUSSION GROUPS

For each topic; Diversity, National Culture, Gender, Generations, Inclusion, LGBT and people with disabilities

- o What stood out to you? Was there a story that you connected with? Why?
- o What did you learn?
- o What similarities do you see in your own life or around you?

Share your response to the questions at the end of each chapter:

- o Introduction: What is your story? Why are you where you are? What made you make these choices?
- o Diversity: What about you, where do you see the benefits of diversity in your surroundings?
- o National culture: What is your national culture(s)? How does it show up at work and in your relationships with people of other cultures? What have you become *blind to* in your own culture?
- o Gender: What can you do to encourage equality for women and men around you?
- o Generations: (On the descriptions of the various generations): What do you recognise? What are your own challenges with working with other generations ? What would make it a learning experience?

- Inclusion
  - What can I do to influence my surroundings towards more inclusion, respect for others and equal/fair treatment?
  - What does my company do, what could be improved?
  - Do I share talking space? How much do I speak and how much do I listen?
  - Do I show respect of others' opinions?
  - How is my body language, and do I keep eye contact with everyone when in a group setting?
  - What do I do if someone uses demeaning language in front of someone I know or tells a stereotyped joke?
  - Do I ask all of my colleagues to go for lunch ? Do I invite my colleagues in another country for a *virtual coffee chat*?
  - As a manager; do I listen to all, do I share information with all, do I encourage ideas, do I invite people to talk ?
  - In my team and in team meetings; do we *talk about how to talk* ?

What else? What would you include?

CHAPTER TEN: TOOLKIT: INCLUSIONAL ACTIVITIES FOR REFLECTION

Having facilitated a few meetings and delivered a few training sessions/workshops in my time, there are some activities I like more than others. These four exercises are among my favourites.

Understanding your own culture

Understanding oneself is key to understand how we engage with others. This is an exercise that can be part of training or a team meeting.

Write up various values on post-its or a board (at least twenty) and ask;

o Identify five values that represent you best as an individual.
- Which one is your *fundamental* or *core* value?
- Which is the most important value in your work day?

o Can people *see* your values in the way you behave? If yes, in what way?
o Can one recognise your five values in the way you manage other people (or work with other people)?

This exercise is first done individually and then discussed in pairs. For a continued discussion in plenary, I suggest the following questions:

o How easy or difficult was this for you? Any surprises?
o Discuss your result and compare: What did you talk about? What did

you have in common?
o Your individual and corporate values .... is there is a difference ?
o Do the chosen words represent your reality or your aspirations? (The values are a mixture of both, they become a reality when your behavior reflects the value)

Tip: Search on Internet for ideas on various values, for example write 'value cards'.

Understanding others

Draw two icebergs on a flipchart, split them in two; writing "behaviour" above and "values" underneath the waterline. Ask;

o What is a behaviour you have that can be misunderstood by others? (E.g. direct communication)
o How do others react to this behaviour? (E.g. see it as blunt or rude)
o What is your underlying value to this behaviour? (E.g. honesty)
o Which value do you believe the other person has? (E.g. politeness)

The exercise works well in pairs, and one can shift pairs within the team. For each iceberg you add the behaviour and value of the two people discussing. This is also an ideal situation to ask for feedback from colleagues (or friends), "Which behaviour do I have that you don't understand?" Then discuss your underlying values.

Promoting inclusion and commitment in teams

At the end of a team meeting or a training session, ask everyone to get up and gather in a large circle. Each person will contribute with an activity they will start doing to promote inclusion (e.g. "I will ask a different colleague every day to go for lunch", "I will make sure everyone gets to say their opinion in team meetings", etc). It should be specific and with a clear commitment. The other team members are 'witnesses' and will remind their colleagues of their commitments.

You need one person to be the 'devil's advocate' to make sure people are specific, and avoid statements like "I will try to…" It should be "I will". You use a yarn that is thrown to each member of the team as an invitation to speak. The aim is to end up with a "spider's net" that the lead person can play with when everyone has contributed. At the end, this person stands in the middle and asks; "What does this net symbolize?" There is no right answer. Most people will say that we are all connected and that if you pull the yarn on one side, it has an effect on another, or even the whole team.

Promoting a large in-group

This exercise can be done individually or as part of a team meeting. It's based on using one's own experience to explore empathy and promote a large *in-group* at work (can also work well with your children and the environment at school).

- o Think about a situation where you were a minority, or someone who felt like an outsider.
- o What type of situation was it? How did you feel?
- o What happened? What did you do?

Based on this experience, what learning can you bring into the work environment? What action can you take that make people feel included and part of the *in-group*?

ABOUT THE AUTHOR

Sunniva Heggertveit-Aoudia is currently working as a consultant, facilitator, mentor and coach (Certified Professional Co-Active Coach - CPCC, and Associate Certified Coach - ACC). She specializes within the areas of Diversity and Inclusion, working with large enterprises across Europe on activities such as reciprocal mentoring, inclusive leadership and cross-cultural intelligence. As a coach she works with medium-sized companies in Europe, as well as individual clients across three continents. Sunniva is also a volunteer member of the board in the Marseille-Provence chapter of the Professional Women's Network (PWN), where she currently has the role of Mentoring Manager.

Sunniva started her career in the travel and tourism industry, then moved on to become a professional recruiter, which became a way into Human Resources. She worked a decade in a large international enterprise, where she had various roles at regional and global levels within Human Resources and Diversity & Inclusion. The D&I jobs inspired her to concentrate full time on these subjects, which she has done as self-employed since 2010.

A Norwegian national, Sunniva lives with her French husband in Southern France. She has two stepsons (in Toulouse and Miami), and two four-legged "children". Sunniva has also lived and worked in Switzerland, Cyprus and the USA. A traveler at heart, she has visited numerous countries and continents, and continues exploring new places with her husband, enjoying the sights, the food and the differences.

ACKNOWLEDGMENTS

Professional

- The story sharers, thank you all for your willingness and openness: Lesley Brook (UK), Ozozoma Sokoh (Nigeria), Kurt Lerbo (Norway), Samira Abbadi (The Netherlands), Thais and Sebastien (France), Lasse Ostervold (Norway), Bart Romanow (Poland), Dana-Leigh Strauss (UK) - also thank you for healthy challenge, and Devika Eifert (Canada) - also thank you for linguistic input and strong support.
- The photo models, thank you for your flexibility, enthusiasm and positive attitude: Photographer and image editor Delphine Baron (France), house dog Ben (UK heritage, French citizenship), house cat Shrek (Unknown heritage, French citizenship)
- Language editor Simon Marshall-Jones (UK): for speedy responses and your respect for the author's writing style.
- Photographer Eric Héranval (France): for priceless expert input!
- Jacqueline Akinyi McMenamin (UK): for clever ideas and challenges.
- Debbie Berger (US): for professional opinion, ideas and support.
- Fiona Morden (UK): for important input at the very beginning of the writing process.
- Asma Al-Ghabshi (Oman): for wise comments.

Family

- My husband: for believing in me.
- My mother: for encouragement and enthusiasm. *She passed away suddenly, only a few weeks after I published the e-version of this book. Seeing it printed next to my mother on her death bed, I decided there would be a paper version within a matter of months.*
- My father: for showing he thinks it's possible.
- My two brothers: for letting me feel that it's just "natural" that their sister should publish a book!
- My dear friend Tove: for loving support.

Thank you also to all the additional friends, family members and colleagues around this globe who made a whole "pom-pom team" of cheerleaders, supporting me all the way!

REFERENCES AND LINKS OF INTEREST

Books:

- "Obliquity. Why Our Goals Are Best Achieved Indirectly". John Kay. 2010. Profile Books Ltd.
- "CI. Cultural Intelligence. The Art of Leading Cultural Complexity". Elisabeth Plum, in collaboration with Benedikte Achen, Inger Draeby, Iben Jensen. 2008. Middlesex University Press.
- "Riding the Waves of Culture. Understanding Diversity in Global Business." Second Edition. Fons Trompenaars and Charles Hampden-Turner. 1998. McGraw-Hill Companies.
- "When Cultures Collide. Leading Across Cultures". Third Edition (2006). Richard D. Lewis. Nicholas Brealey Publishing.
- "Gudinnens fortellinger. Gjemte og glemte skatter i myter og eventyr". (Translation from Norwegian: The goddesses' stories. Forgotten and hidden treasures in myths and fairytales.) Marit Clementz and Ingvild Forbord. 2008. Emilia Press AS.
- "Diversity at Work. The Business Case for Equity". Trevor Wilson. 1997. John Wiley & Sons Canada Limited.

Web sites:

- "Holy Warriors: Islam and the Demise of Classical Civilization". John J. O'Neill. 2009. Felib@ri Publications. Author has used comments refering to his book on the website www.islam-watch.org.
- "Blind men & elephant parable ". Summary made by the association Wild Equus - Equilibre: Understanding horses and horsemanship: http://wildequus.org. Twitter: Victor Ros @equilibregaia
- IMD Business School in Lausanne, text and video from Prof. Maznevski about diverse teams: http://www.imd.org/news/IMD-on-FT-dot-com.cfm
- Stanford Business Graduate School; "Diversity and Work Group Performance: http://www.gsb.stanford.edu/insights/diversity-work-group-performance
- Harvard Business Review : Why Your Brain Loves Good Storytelling, Paul J. Zak: hbr.org/2014/10/why-your-brain-loves-good-storytelling
- Financial Times Special Report: The Inclusive Workplace: http://www.ft.com/intl/recruitment/inclusive-workplace

- The research company Catalyst: http://www.catalyst.org: "Different Cultures; Similar Perceptions", 2006and "Engaging Men in Gender Initiatives", Part 1, 2009
- The Economist; "A Nordic Mystery" : http://www.economist.com/news/business/21632512-worlds-most-female-friendly-workplaces-executive-suites-are-still-male-dominated
- Qur'an verses 33:59; www.quran.com, Surat Al-'Ahzab (The Combined Forces).
- World Economic Forum: The Global Gender Gap report 2014: http://www3.weforum.org/docs/GGGR14/GGGR_CompleteReport_2014.pdf
- Dr. Catherine Hakim, London School of Economics : "Women's 'double shift' of work and domestic duties a myth finds new research" http://www.lse.ac.uk/newsAndMedia/news/archives/2010/08/domestic_duties.aspx
- TEDx talk by Jean Kilbourne on "Killing us softly" : https://www.youtube.com/watch?v=Uy8yLaoWybk
- TEDx talk by Caroline Hedman on "The Sexy Lie" : http://tedxtalks.ted.com/video/The-Sexy-Lie-Caroline-Heldman-a
- Fastcompany.com: "Why you need to stop bragging about how busy you are": http://www.fastcompany.com/3029294/work-smart/why-you-need-to-stop-bragging-about-how-busy-you-are
- Reference to the 2011 ILO (International Labour Organization) report on "Nordic Labour Journal": http://www.nordiclabourjournal.org/nyheter/news-2013/article.2013-04-08.8112434876
- "The U-Bend of Life", The Economist: http://www.economist.com/node/17722567
- Carole Kauffmann on Positive Psychology: The Science at the Heart of Coaching: The Institute of Coaching: http://www.instituteofcoaching.org/images/pdfs/Evidence-based-Coaching-PositivePsychology.pdf
- Ladder of Inference, explanation by "MindTools": http://www.mindtools.com/pages/article/newTMC_91.htm
- Dr. Edward Hubbard, The Business Case for Diversity : http://www.multiculturaladvantage.com/recruit/metrics/The-Business-Case-for-Diversity.asp
- LGBT data: Harris Interactive: http://www.harrisinteractive.com/NewsRoom/PressReleases/tabid/446/mid/1506/articleId/835/ctl/ReadCustom%20Default/Default.aspx
- Video: Growing up gay; Brian McNaught: Can be bought on: http://www.brian-mcnaught.com/books/growingupgay.htm

- o   Data on disability, Australia: http://www.and.org.au/pages/disability-statistics.html
- o   French data on people with hearing impairment: Union Nationale des Associations de Parents d'Enfants Déficients Auditifs: http://www.unapeda.asso.fr
- o   Norwegian consulting company focusing on autism-positive characteristics: UNICUS: http://unicus.no/en/about/

Links that might be of interest to the reader

- o   Story-sharer Lesley Brook, link to company: www.brookgraham.com
- o   Story-sharer Ozozoma Sokoh, link to her blog: http://www.kitchenbutterfly.com/ - and her TEDx talk "Journey by Plate": https://www.youtube.com/watch?v=TiSluxo1Bds
- o   Story-sharer Samira Abbadi; link to company: http://www.debaak.com and to the Rotterdam event: http://djemaaelfnarotterdam.stichtingdeloodsen.nl
- o   Story sharer Lasse Ostervold; polar bear visit: https://www.youtube.com/watch?v=cfR0H-bBA4A
- o   YouTube link on "Power of Words": https://www.youtube.com/watch?v=p48xtb80WRU
- o   The Center for Talent Innovation: http://www.talentinnovation.org
- o   CatchAFire (site for volunteers): https://www.catchafire.org
- o   Project Implicit by Harvard (unconscious bias): https://implicit.harvard.edu/implicit/
- o   Ni Putes Ni Soumises: http://www.npns.fr
- o   UN's campaign HeForShe: http://www.heforshe.org

Images: Photos

- o   Map of Norway: Avinor/lufthavnkart: http://www.avinor.no/avinor/lufthavnkart
- o   Nordic flags: Nordic Studies Website http://www.stolaf.edu/depts/norwegian/nordic/colleges/
- o   Pixabay: http://pixabay.com (free images)
- o   Wikimedia Commons: https://commons.wikimedia.org (free media files)
- o   Private photos by author and photo editor

Images: Graphs

- Data on immigration in Europe drawn from European Commision's site "eurostat": File: Immigrants, 2012 (1) (per 1 000 inhabitants) YB14 II.png:http://ec.europa.eu/eurostat/statistics-explained/index.php/File:Immigrants,_2012_(1)_(per_1_000_inhabitants)_YB14_II.png#
- Data on female self-employent, drawn from OECD: https://data.oecd.org/emp/self-employment-rate.htm
- Data on women and men on boards 2014, drawn from from European Commission: http://ec.europa.eu/justice/gender-equality/gender-decision-making/database/business-finance/supervisory-board-board-directors/index_en.htm
- Data on mental disability and employment, drawn from OECD: http://www.oecd.org/employment/emp/theoecdmentalhealthandworkproject.htm

Made in the USA
Charleston, SC
02 October 2015